The Consequences of Sin

The Consequences of Sin

by

John MacArthur, Jr.

MOODY PRESS

CHICAGO

ISBN: 0-8024-5109-8

2 3 4 5 6 7 Printing/EP/Year 91 90 89 88 87 86

Printed in the United States of America

Contents

These Bible studies are taken from messages delivered by Pastor-Teacher John MacArthur, Jr., at Grace Community Church in Panorama City, California. The recorded messages themselves may be purchased as a series or individually. Please request the current price list by writing to:

WORD OF GRACE COMMUNICATIONS
P.O. Box 4000
Panorama City, CA 91412

Or call the following toll-free number:
1-800-55-GRACE

1

The Attitude Behind the Act

Outline

Introduction
A. Man's Evaluation of the Appearance
B. God's Emphasis of the Attitude
    1. Identified in the Scriptures
        a) Matthew 5:20
        b) 1 Kings 8:39
        c) 1 Chronicles 28:9*a*
    2. Clarified by the Savior

Lesson
I. The Passage Examined
   A. Its Illustrations Identified
   B. The Context Clarified
      1. The lowering of the standard
      2. The lifting of the standard
   C. Its Authority Amplified
      1. The possibilities examined
      2. The preference explained
      3. The practice exemplified
         a) By the Roman Catholic church before the Reformation
         b) By the Jews after the Babylonian captivity
      4. The perplexity expressed
         a) The respect of the Lord
         b) The reverence of the law
II. The Principles Expressed
   A. Regarding the Law
      1. Its priority
         a) Explained
         b) Exemplified
      2. Its positiveness
      3. Its purpose
   B. Regarding the Lawgiver
      1. His discernment
      2. His demands

a) In the words of Jesus

b) In the words of Paul

Conclusion

Introduction

A. Man's Evaluation of the Appearance

Most people evaluate their lives and the lives of other people on the basis of external appearance. First Samuel 16:7 says, "For man looketh on the outward appearance." Jesus says in John 7:24, "Judge not according to the appearance, but judge righteous judgment." In 2 Corinthians 10:7 and 12, Paul says, "Do ye look on things after the outward appearance? . . . For we dare not make ourselves of the number, or compare ourselves with some that commend themselves." In other words, there are people who commend themselves on the basis of their outward appearance. There are people who are satisfied with how they behave externally. And there are people who evaluate others on the basis of what they see in terms of religious behavior. Such evaluation is rather typical of fallen man—he is basically satisfied with externals.

B. God's Emphasis of the Attitude

God is not so concerned with the outside as much as He is with the inside. The outside is only validated insofar as it is representative of what is on the inside. This principle is the basis of the text that we shall consider. Jesus emphasizes here in the Sermon on the Mount and throughout the rest of His ministry that external ceremonies and religious rites are not the important issue, because God's primary concern is with the heart. That is precisely the thrust which is:

1. Identified in the Scriptures

a) Matthew 5:20—"For I say unto you that except your righteousness shall exceed the righteousness of the scribes and Pharisees, ye shall in no case enter into the kingdom of heaven." The scribes and the Pharisees had a righteousness that was external, and Jesus was saying that you must have one which exceeds that—one which is internal. God is concerned about what you really are—not what you appear to be. It is the internal that is infinitely more important than the external. Whereas the righteousness of the scribes and the Pharisees was an external, ceremonial, ritualistic, hypocritical legalism, the righteousness that God demands is something internal. That has always been God's concern. Jesus was not articulating something never before known.

b) 1 Kings 8:39—"Then hear thou in heaven, thy dwelling place, and forgive, and do, and give to every man according to his ways, whose heart thou knowest (for thou, even thou only, knowest the hearts of all the children of men)." God is enjoined in that verse to respond to men not on the basis of outward deeds, but on the basis of the heart which He alone knows.

c) 1 Chronicles 28:9*a*—"And thou, Solomon, my son, know thou the God of thy father, and serve him with a perfect heart and with a willing mind; for the Lord searcheth all hearts, and understandeth all the imaginations of the thoughts." God is more concerned with the inside than the outside.

The standard that God sets to evaluate men and women is the standard of the heart. The message is clear: Though God is concerned with external behavior, that behavior is only justified insofar as it is the outgrowth of internal righteousness, for God evaluates the heart. The need for the internal righteousness that God requires was:

2. Clarified by the Savior

At this point in the Sermon on the Mount in Matthew 5, Jesus shows how people living by such a principle relate to the Old Testament law, because such an understanding is critical to the Jews listening to Him speak. What He has been saying so far has been revolutionary to them, because they have a purely external religion. Because the truths He has laid down are not common to their understanding of religion, they would have questions like, "This may be well and good, but how does it relate to the Old Testament, and to Moses, and to what the rabbis have taught? How does it relate to the system of traditional law that we adhere to?" The Jews to whom Jesus was preaching would lean so completely on the teachings related to their own Judaistic law, that our Lord couldn't bypass this section in verses 21 through 48. He has to show how this relates to their system. Verse 20 becomes the key as He says, "God's standard is higher than yours. What you now know as a righteous standard is unacceptable."

Now immediately they're going to say, "Wait a minute! We obey the law of God." But Jesus is saying, "Not at all. In fact, I have to redefine the law of God for you, because it's been lost in the midst of your tradition." The Judaism of the time was far from that true Old Testament law which God had given. This is how Jesus could say in verses 17 and 18, "Think not that I am come to destroy the law, or the prophets. . . . Till heaven and earth pass, one jot or one tittle shall in no way pass from the law." In other words, "I'm not going to tolerate anybody who sets aside one of God's commands. What you have is not God's law; therefore, I must redefine it for you." And this is exactly what He does through the rest of chapters 5 through 7. They contain Jesus' explanation of what He said in verses 17 through 20 of Matthew 5.

Now, let's begin to see how Jesus goes about this in chapter 5.

Lesson

I. THE PASSAGE EXAMINED

A. Its Illustrations Identified

Beginning in verse 21, we find a phrase that is repeated several times throughout the chapter: "Ye have heard that it was said by them of old . . . but I say unto you—" Watch for it in the following verses. "Ye have heard that it was said by them of old, Thou shalt not kill and whosoever shall kill shall be in danger of judgment; but I say unto you that whosoever is angry with his brother without a cause shall be in danger of judgment" (vv. 21-22*a*). "Ye have heard that it was said by them of old, Thou shalt not commit adultery; but I say unto you that whosoever looketh on a woman to lust after her hath committed adultery with her already in his heart" (vv. 27-28). "It hath been said, Whosoever shall put away his wife, let him give her a writing of divorcement; but I say unto you that whosoever shall put away his wife, except for the cause of fornication, causeth her to commit adultery" (vv. 31-32*a*). "Again, ye have heard that it hath been said by them of old, Thou shalt not perjure thyself, but shalt perform unto the Lord thine oaths; but I say unto you, Swear not at all" (vv. 33-34*a*). "Ye have heard that it hath been said, An eye for an eye, and a tooth for a tooth; but I say unto you that ye resist not evil, but whosoever shall smite thee on thy right cheek, turn to him the other also" (vv. 38-39). "Ye have heard that it hath been said, Thou shalt love thy neighbor, and hate thine enemy; but I say unto you, Love your enemies" (vv. 43-44*a*).

B. The Context Clarified

1. The lowering of the standard

These six specific illustrations all follow a similar pattern. Jesus is saying, "Your religion teaches you that, but I say that you should do this." Jesus is not comparing Himself with the Old Testament. He's not raising the standard higher than the law of God. He's not talking about what Moses said. Jesus is talking about what their religious system taught them. He's saying, "Your standard is too low. You only worry about murder, while God looks at the heart and says if there's hate there, it's the same thing. You only worry about fornication, while God says that if there's lust in the heart, it's the same thing. God's standard is an attitudinal standard—yours is only dealing with action. That's the difference. The internal things are what God is really looking for."

In selecting His illustrations, Jesus is very careful. First of all, He chooses two commands from the Decalogue, or the Ten Commandments, given by Moses: "Thou shalt not kill [murder]" (Ex. 20:13), and "thou shalt not commit adultery" (Ex. 20:14). Then, He chooses two other commandments, taken from other portions of the Mosaic writings, which are more general and deal with social relationships. Finally, He broadens to discuss the whole subject of love. In effect, what Jesus is saying is that God has standards, such as those regarding murder and adultery, that affect the very foundation of a society—the individual and the family. Beyond those basic standards are ones that relate to a wider set of social relationships, involving the issues of truth and justice. And finally, Jesus says that God's standards extend to the attitude of love, which affects the widest possible category of society, including even enemies. In other words, in all aspects of life, from the individual, to the family, to social relationships, to the wider world of our enemies, we should be characteristically righteous on the inside—a righteousness that affects not only behavioral standards in terms of what we do, but also in terms of what we think.

2. The lifting of the standard

The religious system of that day didn't have that definition, because it was strictly external. Therefore, when Jesus said that one's righteousness must exceed the righteousness of the scribes and Pharisees to be pleasing to God, His listeners were immediately shocked. But don't think for a minute that Jesus Christ came to set aside the law of God. He came to strip the rabbinic barnacles off the law of God to make it as pure as it was when God gave it by lifting it back to where it belonged. God had always been concerned with attitudes—that wasn't anything new. It was just that the people of Israel had lowered the standard and consequently needed to be reminded of that. They were justifying themselves by what they didn't do, while their hearts were full of murder, lust, lies, hate, and anger. To appear righteous, they were forced to lower the standards to accommodate their sin. This is why Jesus lifted it right back where it belonged, emphasizing that thoughts are just as important as deeds.

Such a confrontation was literally devastating to the Pharisees, because Jesus saw through their externals and exposed their hearts as being rotten. In fact, later on in Matthew 23, He says, "Outside you're whitewashed, inside you're like a tomb full of dead men's bones" (v. 27). Jesus made it plain that men and women are not to be judged solely by their deeds and actions, but by their desires and attitudes as well. This is as different from the world's standards today as it was for the scribes and Pharisees, who saw a man or woman as righteous if they never did the forbidden things. They didn't care about their thoughts or attitudes. In contrast, Jesus said that a man is righteous if he never desires the forbidden things.

Patrick Fairbairn has written some words that are worth noting: "In the revelation of law there was a substratum of grace, recognized in the words which prefaced the Ten Commandments, and promises of grace in blessing also intermingled with the stern prohibitions and injunctions of which they consist. And so, inversely in the Sermon on the Mount, while it gives grace the priority and the prominence, it is far from excluding the severer part of God's character and government. No sooner, indeed, had grace poured itself forth in a succession of beatitudes, than there appeared the stern demands of righteousness and law."

God is not saying that if you are a Christian, you're free to do whatever you want. He is saying that for a child of the kingdom, the standard is raised rather than lowered. The standards are still there, because the God who examines the heart hasn't changed.

Who is qualified to judge?

A key passage that answers this question is 1 Corinthians 4:3-5, where Paul addresses the issue of the Corinthians' criticism of his ministry.

1. Refusing human evaluation (v. 3)

   "But with me it is a very small thing that I should be judged of you, or of man's judgment; yea, I judge not mine own self."

   Paul is saying, "Look, I will not allow myself to settle for human evaluation. I won't do it. Not yours and not mine." I can identify with that, because I tend to be biased in my own favor, which is a rather typical human response. Sometimes people will give me gracious compliments, and though I appreciate them, it is not really important to me how I am evaluated by others, especially critics. The reason that I don't readily accept human evaluation, including my own, is that whether it is critical or kind, neither of us really know the secrets of the heart. I may know a little more than you, but even I don't know the whole picture.

2. Recognizing honest justification (v. 4)

   "For I know nothing against myself, yet am I not hereby justified; but he that judgeth me is the Lord."

   In other words, Paul is saying, "Though there's nothing in my life I can see that is wrong, that doesn't justify me. That's the Lord's job." We may be able to see the externals, but they are not always good indicators of what's going on inside. A "good" action may be interpreted as being bad or just the reverse, as the following incident shows.

   I'll never forget one time when I was in a college where they had so many rules you couldn't even read them in a whole year. It was possible to break rules you didn't even know existed. On one occasion, a guy was called to the high tribunal of this school and was told, "You have broken the cardinal rule: We saw you leaving the campus with a blonde in a blue dress sitting next to you in your car. Where were you going?" Now in this particular school, you couldn't go anywhere with a girl, let alone leave the campus in your car. So, this was a horrendous crime of the first order. To this accusation, the young man replied, "That was my blue laundry bag and hanging out of it was a yellow towel!" Unfortunately, by that time, the rumor was already spread far and wide: This dissolute young man had been seen driving around with a blonde in a blue dress.

3. Revealing hidden motivation (v. 5)

   "Therefore, judge nothing before the time, until the Lord come, who both will bring to light the hidden things of darkness, and will make manifest the counsels [motives] of the hearts."

When God judges righteous judgment, He judges motives. You may be one who goes through life and never strikes a blow to anyone. You may have never killed anybody or even fought with anybody, but you may literally burn inside with anger. You may be one who's never been unfaithful in your marriage, but you cultivate the thoughts of adultery repeatedly. You may be one who's never perjured yourself in a court of law, and yet your word is not really your bond— you don't always follow through with the things you have promised. These inner things cannot escape the scrutiny of God. You may want so badly to commit a sin, and though you never actually do it, God still holds you accountable as if you had. God judges the evil desire.

Jesus was literally hitting these Pharisees right between the eyes. Their hearts were filthy, while their deeds were religious. As Patrick Fairbairn has well said, "The scribes and Pharisees of that age had completely inverted the order of things. Their carnality and self-righteousness had led them to exalt the precepts respecting ceremonial observances to the highest place, and to throw the duties inculcated in the Ten Commandments comparatively into the background." They just dealt with externals. But though the state of the heart was not their concern, it was Jesus' concern. Look at our own society. People do this very thing all the time: "Oh, so-and-so is such a good person. He's so charitable." Yet God knows what's going on inside—only He knows the motives behind what we do.

C. Its Authority Amplified

  1. The possibilities examined

    There is a slight variation in the form of the phrase that's repeated in this passage, but it is basically the same in each of the six incidents. There are two possibilities with regard to how the phrase could be translated. It could read, "Ye have heard that it was said *to* them of old" or "*by* them of old." The Greek could be translated either way. If the phrase used the word *to,* it would probably refer to the Old Testament. But if the word *by* was used, this would indicate that it isn't the Bible speaking to the people, but some ancient people speaking.

  2. The preference explained

    I believe that the proper rendering is "*by* them of old" for several reasons: I don't think the law of Moses is in view, because Jesus isn't saying, "You have heard that it was said to them of old by Moses or by God, but I'm saying this," or He would be contradicting the words of Moses from God in the Old Testament. Furthermore, if Jesus had said that, He would be setting aside the law and the prophets, which would be a direct contradiction of what He had just said in verse 17. Another reason I don't think that Moses was the one being referred to is that Jesus did not say, "You have heard that Moses commanded," or, "You have heard that it is written," which is precisely what He says three times in Matthew 4 when He refers to the Old Testament. And in chapter 8, when He refers to the Old Testament, He says, "Moses commanded." The last reason for not accepting "to" as the best translation is the fact that famous rabbis were called "fathers of antiquity" or "men of long ago." Hence, I believe this is what our Lord is referring to: "You have heard that it was said by the rabbis of old." In other words, this is a designation related to their oral teaching that glossed over the true law of God, as they added their own thoughts to the revelation of the Old Testament. So Jesus is not contrasting the Old Testament with the New Testament or His word with God's word, but the word of the rabbis and their traditional interpretation which had been given to the people. Let me give you two illustrations of this that Martyn Lloyd-Jones has used:

3. The practice exemplified

   a) By the Roman Catholic church before the Reformation

      The condition of the Jew at the time of Christ was remarkably like that of the people in the Reformation. Prior to the Reformation, the Scriptures were not translated into the people's language. When you went to church for the mass, the whole thing was done in Latin. There was no Bible to speak of in the hands of the people. The only contact the people had with the Bible was from what was read by the priests in Latin. Consequently, nobody understood it, and nobody read it except the priests, who would expound upon this Latin text. The people would simply believe whatever the priest said because they had no basis by which to evaluate. They couldn't read the Latin, let alone interpret it. So they accepted what the priest said.

      Century after century went by in this way, with the Roman Catholic church having developed a system that was never really investigated by the people, mainly because they didn't have the Bible in their own language. The people had unquestioningly accepted the priestly interpretations and conformity to the system of Rome. What the Reformation did more than anything else was give the Bible to the people. It put the Word of God in the people's hands. When they began to read the Scripture, then many began to see the false teaching and the misrepresentation of the gospel that had been given to them for centuries. It was the truth of the gospel that helped to shatter the Dark Ages, and Protestant Christianity as we know it today was born out of that. And today, we have the Bible in our own languages and are therefore able to evaluate the validity of any religious system by the Bible's divine standard.

This was the kind of thing that was going on in our Lord's day. Another similar illustration can be found:

b) By the Jews after the Babylonian captivity

When Israel went into captivity for seventy years, historians tell us that they essentially lost the Hebrew language, acquiring instead a language known as Aramaic. Consequently, when they came back from captivity, the Jews were still speaking Aramaic up to, and beyond, the time of Jesus. Because the Jewish people spoke Aramaic and were, for the most part, completely unfamiliar with Hebrew, the people were dependent upon the rabbis to read and interpret the Hebrew language, which the people didn't understand. Thus, the rabbis began to build an entire system based upon the ignorance of the people regarding the Hebrew text.

As a result of this situation, the Lord is best understood as having said, "Ye have heard that it was said by them of old." In this case, He would be describing the religion of the Jews at that time as a product of the oral tradition of the rabbis, rather than from the written Word of God. Their religious system had departed from its biblical base with all of the embellishments, traditions, and interpretations of the Mishnah (the codification of oral law) and the rest of the Talmud, which, in effect, pushed the truth of God into obscurity. Partly for this reason, our Lord came along saying, "I am here to loose the law of God from the shackles of rabbinic mishmash." Most significantly, He attacked their emphasis upon external works for righteousness, saying, "You have heard it said by them of old, but I say unto you—"

4. The perplexity expressed

a) The respect of the Lord

With this phrase, Jesus established Himself as the authority. When He said, "I will tell you what God's law really is," the people were shocked. In fact, they said of Him that "he taught them as one that had authority, and not as the scribes" (Mark 1:22*b*). Similarly, in Matthew 7, as He concluded His sermon, "the people were astonished at his doctrine; for he taught them as one having authority, and not as the scribes" (vv. 28*b*-29).

b) The reverence of the law

They were shocked for someone to set himself as equal to the law of God, because the Jews believed that this traditional law that they assumed to be the law of God was sacred. For example, Philo said, "Only Moses' decrees are everlasting, unchangable, unshakable." The rabbis said, "Those who deny that the law is from heaven have no part in the world to come." They believed this was the only law and that eternal destiny was dependent upon it. But here came along Jesus, and He spoke without ever quoting a rabbi. When He gave His own authoritative statement, the people were literally shocked, for He was claiming equal authority to the law they so greatly reverenced. Whereas the prophets always said, "Thus saith the Lord," and the rabbis said, "There is a teaching that says," Jesus said, "I say unto you." Rightly did William Barclay remark, "Clearly one of two things must be true—either Jesus was mad, or He was unique; either He was a megalomaniac or else He was the Son of God." No ordinary person would dare to claim what He claimed. Jesus clearly claimed the authority of God, stripping away the layers of tradition that concealed God's true law and lifting it back to where it belonged.

Now, let me close the introduction to this passage by summarizing the key principles Jesus is teaching here.

II. THE PRINCIPLES EXPRESSED

A. Regarding the Law

1. Its priority

It is the spirit of the law that is the priority, not the letter.

a) Explained

The law is not mechanical or simply functional. However, when it is misused in this way, it is possible to be all white on the outside and a wretched, vile grave on the inside. Knowing that it is the letter of the law that kills and the Spirit that gives life (2 Cor. 3:6), we must realize that God is not looking for externals—He's looking for changed hearts. The scribes and Pharisees thought that because they didn't murder or commit adultery, they were all right—but they were hateful and harbored lustful thoughts. Their religion was a legalistic hypocrisy of the worst kind—one that damned the soul. It failed to teach that conformity to God's law is a matter of the heart and not simply a matter of the outside.

b) Exemplified

Oh, what a lesson this is to us who tend to justify ourselves! In Luke 16:15 Jesus says to the Pharisees, "Ye are they who justify yourselves before men, but God knoweth your hearts; for that which is highly esteemed among men is abomination in the sight of God." Men and God judge differently. You can come to church, and you can play the game, talk the talk, do the works in the energy of the flesh, justifying yourself in your own eyes and in the eyes of others, and at the same time be an abomination to God because your heart is full of corruption. That's what Jesus was saying. Truly it is the spirit of the law that is the priority, not the letter.

2. Its positiveness

The law is not just negative, it is also positive.

The law of God is not just to prevent us from doing certain things; its real object is to lead us to right attitudes. It is a positive thing. The Pharisees were concerned with what they didn't do. God was concerned with what they did do inside. Did they hunger and thirst after righteousness? Did they seek to be merciful? Were they pure in heart? Did they mourn over their sin? Were they poor in spirit? Were they peacemakers? That's what God was concerned with—the development of spiritual character.

3. Its purpose

The law is not an end in itself.

It had a purpose. What is the goal of the law? The Pharisees said that it was to glorify me when I keep the law so that people could see how righteous I am. But the true end of the law is to glorify God. It's not a question of asking yourself, "Have I kept all the laws today?" but rather, "Have I glorified God in my spirit today? Have I been free from phoniness? Have I had a pure heart that had no thought of evil, anger, hatred, bitterness, lust, or unrighteousness—to the glory of God?"

John Calvin made this tremendous statement in his *Institutes:* "First, let us agree that through the law man's life is molded not only to outward honesty but to inward and spiritual righteousness. Although no one can deny this, very few duly note it. This happens because they do not look to the Lawgiver, by whose character the nature of the law is to be appraised. If some king by edict forbids fornication, murder, or theft, I admit that a man who does not commit such acts will not be bound by the penalty. That is because the moral lawgiver's jurisdiction extends only to the outward political order. . . . But God, whose eye nothing escapes, and who is concerned not so much with outward appearance as with purity of heart, forbids not only fornication, murder, theft—but lust, anger, hatred, coveting . . . deceit. . . . For since He is a spiritual lawgiver, He speaks no less to the soul than to the body" (*Library of Christian Classics* [Philadelphia: Westminster, 1967], vol. 1, p. 372). What Calvin means is, if you think God's laws are only external, then you don't know the character of God.

Next, we come to the first two principles:

B. Regarding the Lawgiver

1. His discernment

   God alone can judge men.

   He alone sees the secrets of the heart. He knows you—and He knows if you're really a Christian or if you're playing a religious game. He knows if you're carnal or spiritual as a believer. He knows whether it's just a matter of acts or really of attitudes. He knows whether or not the heart matches the outside. Hebrews 4:12-13 says, "For the word of God is living, and powerful . . . and is a discerner of the thoughts and intents of the heart. Neither is there any creature that is not manifest in his sight, but all things are naked and opened unto the eyes of him with whom we have to do." But though God knows everything, we can find comfort in the fact that we have a faithful, sympathetic high priest: "Let us, therefore, come boldly unto the throne of grace, that we may obtain mercy, and find grace to help in time of need" (v. 16). Isn't it great? God knows our hearts. He knows if they're rotten, but He stands with His arms open, ready to give us grace and mercy. God alone can judge the heart. Though many a man and woman can stand the judgment of men, they will fall before the discerning eye of God. You had better examine your own heart.

19

2. His demands

Every person is commanded to live up to divine standards.

a) In the words of Jesus

"For I say unto you that except your righteousness shall exceed the righteousness of the scribes and Pharisees, ye shall in no case enter into the kingdom of heaven. . . . Be ye, therefore, perfect, even as your Father, who is in heaven, is perfect" (Matt. 5:20, 48).

Every person in the world is required to live up to that standard. You say, "You've got to be kidding!" No, I'm not. You are obligated to live up to that standard with a pure inside as well as a right outside. But you say, "I can't!" You are absolutely right. That's why we are given the solution.

b) In the words of Paul

"As it is written, There is none righteous, no, not one. . . . But now the righteousness of God apart from the law is manifested, being witnessed by the law and the prophets, even the righteousness of God which is by faith of Jesus Christ unto all and upon all them that believe" (Rom. 3:10, 21-22*a*).

Though you can't obtain on your own the righteous standard Christ set, you can receive His righteousness if you are one of those who believe. God set the holy standard. And when you acknowledge that you can't live up to it, He says, "My Son is not only the Lawgiver, but He is the Redeemer as well, who makes it possible for you to live on that level." It's a fantastic thing! The standard is so high we can't attain it. But Christ met that standard and imputes to us His righteousness. Oh, what a blessed thing!

Conclusion

You may look at yourself and say, "The outside is not bad, but the inside is rotten." And if God did what was right, He would consume you in a blast of His fury. But because He's a merciful and gracious God, He makes His Lawgiver not just a lawgiver, but a Redeemer, too. Jesus, who perfectly kept the law, imputes His righteousness to us so that when God looks at those of us who are believers, He sees the righteousness of Jesus Christ concerning us. I stand before God as righteous as Christ. But you can't even have that gift of righteousness unless you recognize that what you need is that gift of righteousness. As long as you live your life justifying yourself on your external behavior, you will never come to the desperation that reaches out and accepts the gift of righteousness.

The great preacher of many years ago Henry Ward Beecher had a clock in his church that didn't keep good time. It was always too fast or too slow. Month after month he fiddled with it, trying to rectify the problem. Soon it became a standard topic of conversation in the church, until finally in desperation, he put a sign over the clock that said, "Don't blame the hands, the trouble lies deeper." That's how it is in life, isn't it? Don't blame the hands, the trouble lies deeper. And until you deal with the deeper trouble of the spiritual realm, there will be no way to set the hands aright permanently.

Focusing on the Facts

1. On what basis do most people evaluate their own lives, as well as the lives of others (see p. 8)?
2. With what is God primarily concerned (see p. 8)?
3. The _____ is only validated insofar as it is representative of what is on the _____ (see p. 9).
4. Compare the righteousness that the Pharisees had to the kind that God demands (see pp. 8-9).
5. Why did Jesus have to redefine the law of the Judaism of His day (see p. 10)?
6. What is the phrase that Jesus repeats from verses 21-44 of Matthew 5 (see p. 10)?
7. What is the significance of the variety of illustrations that Jesus selected in Matthew 5:21-44 with regard to the degree that we should be characteristically righteous on the inside (see p. 11)?
8. Why did Jesus have to lift the standard of God up (see pp. 11-12)?
9. Why did Paul refuse to accept human evaluation regarding his motives (see p. 13)?
10. Why are externals not always good indicators of what is going on inside (see p. 13)?
11. Who alone knows the motives behind what we do (see pp. 13-14)?
12. If the phrase of Jesus were to be translated "it was said *to* them of old," what would the source of authority be identified as? If the word "by" were used, who would be identified as the ones speaking? What are some reasons that the latter choice is preferred (see pp. 14-15)?
13. Rather than contrasting His word with what God had already revealed in the Old Testament, what was Jesus really comparing His teaching to (see p. 15)?
14. How were the situations of the people before the Reformation and the Jews after the Babylonian captivity similar with regard to the teaching from the Bible (see pp. 15-16)?

15. What was the people's reaction to the teaching of Jesus, according to Matthew 7:28-29 (see p. 17)?
16. To what was Jesus claiming equal authority that shocked the people (see p. 17)?
17. What did the Judaism of Christ's day fail to teach with regard to conformity to God's law (see p. 18)?
18. Rather than just to prevent us from doing certain things, what is the real object of the law, from a positive perspective (see p. 18)?
19. What was the true purpose of the law, as opposed to how the Pharisees used it (see p. 18)?
20. Who is commanded to live up to divine standards? What is the only way that righteous standard can be attributed to us (see p. 20)?

Pondering the Principles

1. What standards do you regulate your life by? Do you accept the Bible as the authoritative Word of God? Or, have you lowered your standards to the degree that anything you do can be justified in your own eyes? If Jesus were to come to you and evaluate your religious activity, would He say that you had maintained His standards, lowered them, or even raised them higher than what He expects? As you read the Bible, do you discover things in your life that don't match up to the biblical mandates? If so, do you just assume that the Bible doesn't match your standard because you are part of a different culture or because of some other reason? Or, do you try to find ways that you can adjust your life to match Scripture? Make a point of finding answers to any discrepancies between what the Bible says and what believers actually do, by consulting Bible teachers and commentaries. You just may find that you or your church might have to begin doing things a little differently.
2. How's your thought life? Knowing that "all things are naked and opened unto the eyes of him with whom we have to do" (Heb. 4:13*b*) and that God's judgment goes behind the action to the attitude, do you consciously make an effort to control the content of your thoughts? Identify those desires you cherish which are not glorifying to God and, after you have confessed them, ask God to strengthen you in "bringing into captivity every thought to the obedience of Christ" (2 Cor. 10:5*b*).
3. This week, keep a mental note of how many times you judge the motives of others that you have no way of really verifying, as well as the times you perform an action with the wrong attitude. You may find that God still needs to do some refining in your life in these areas. If you catch yourself judging the motives of others, think the best of them with the kind of love that "beareth all things, believeth all things, hopeth all things, endureth all things" (1 Cor. 13:7).

2

Who Is a Murderer?

Outline

Introduction
A. Murder in Society
B. Murder in Scripture
  1. Its condemnation
  2. Its consequence
  3. Its constitution
    a) What it is not
    b) What it is
      (1) Punishable by death
      (2) Authored by the devil
      (3) A manifestation of an evil heart
      (4) A result of a reprobate mind
      (5) An act of the flesh
      (6) An abomination to God
      (7) A cause for exclusion from heaven
  4. Its context

Lesson
I. The Effect of Jesus' Words upon the Self-Righteousness of Man
  A. The tradition of the Jews
    1. Emphasizing the externals
    2. Excluding the internals
  B. The teaching of Jesus
    1. The indictment of Jesus
    2. The illustrations of judgment
      a) The sin of anger
        (1) Its exception
        (2) Its explanation
      b) The sin of slander
      c) The sin of cursing
        (1) Its foolish recipient
        (2) Its fiery retribution

Introduction

A. Murder in Society

Murders result from all kinds of conflicts. They come as the result of violent crimes, domestic squabbles, homosexual as well as heterosexual love triangles, gang warfares, and all types of arguments, fights, and misunderstandings. Murders go on all the time. In fact, they are so commonplace in our cities that they don't always make the newspapers, unless they're bizarre or multiple. Murder is a very serious problem in our world—one that is getting worse all the time. And we haven't even mentioned some of its other forms such as suicide or abortion, which alone has resulted in the murder of millions of babies since its legalization.

B. Murder in Scripture

1. Its condemnation

In Matthew 5:21, our Lord says, "Ye have heard that it was said by them of old, Thou shalt not kill." Where did that come from? Well, if you know anything about the revelation of God, you know it came from Exodus 20:13, when God gave the Decalogue and said, "Thou shalt not kill." But Scripture has a lot more to say about murder than just that. If we look at Genesis 9:6, we are informed of:

2. Its consequence

"Whoso sheddeth man's blood, by man shall his blood be shed; for in the image of God made he man." God instituted capital punishment as a penalty for murder, because to take the life of a human being is to assault the image of God He created in man.

3. Its constitution

a) What it is not

If you were to study Exodus 20:13, you would find that the word "kill" means murder. It does not refer to capital punishment, that is, the taking of a life under divine allowance by the hand of those who "beareth not the sword in vain" (Rom. 13:4b). It does not refer to a just war when, in the divine plan of history, there are conflicts on a national level which carry out the will of God in judgment upon some nations. Nor do I believe that the text of Exodus 20:13 has anything to do with self-defense, because we have the right to protect the image of God in our lives and the lives of others when they are assaulted and attacked by those who would kill them. Furthermore, I don't believe it means accidental deaths. In Deuteronomy 19, for example, it says that if a man takes the life of someone inadvertently, then that man is not to forfeit his life, because there was no premeditation involved.

b) What it is

What the Bible is talking about regarding the command to not kill is murder, a planned and plotted act of violence. Scripture tells us that murder is:

(1) Punishable by death

In Exodus 21:14, we read, "But if a man come presumptuously upon his neighbor, to slay him with guile, thou shalt take him from mine altar, that he may die." God reiterates the sentence of capital punishment for the one who premeditates to take the life of his neighbor.

(2) Authored by the devil

John 8:44 says that the devil is a murderer.

(3) A manifestation of an evil heart

In Matthew 15:19, we find that murder is a manifestation of an evil human heart: "For out of the heart proceed evil thoughts, murders, adulteries, fornications, thefts, false witness, blasphemies." Murders, thefts, and all those other things do not happen because of social deprivation or stressful situations; they happen because of a degenerated human heart.

(4) A result of a reprobate mind

In Romans 1:28, it says that man has been given over to a reprobate mind, and, as a result, he is "filled with all unrighteousness, fornication, wickedness, covetousness, maliciousness; full of envy, murder, strife,

25

deceit" (v. 29). Man is a murderer because he has a reprobate mind that has been given over to evil, because he has rejected God.

(5) An act of the flesh

In Galatians 5:21, Paul tells us that murder is a deed done by unregenerated human nature.

(6) An abomination to God

Proverbs 6:16-17 says, "These six things doth the Lord hate; yea, seven are an abomination unto him: a proud look, a lying tongue, and hands that shed innocent blood."

(7) A cause for exclusion from heaven

Revelation 22:14-15 says, "Blessed are they that wash their robes, that they may have right to the tree of life, and may enter in through the gates into the city. For outside are dogs, and sorcerers, and fornicators, and murderers." The kingdom of God in its eternal state is not a place for murderers.

4. Its context

Now, if we get sick inside just thinking about such a crime as murder, we identify well with the scribes and Pharisees that Jesus is speaking to. For in Matthew 5-7, our Lord is addressing the scribes and Pharisees on a hillside in Galilee along with the rest of the multitude, and here He begins to confront their superficial approach to life, saying, "Ye have heard that it was said by them of old, Thou shalt not [murder] and whosoever shall kill shall be in danger of judgment" (5:21). Jesus is saying, "You believe that it is wrong to murder because if you do, you'll be in danger of judgment." And at that point, many of the Jews would have probably been thinking, "Amen! We're against murder; we have been taught by them of old according to the rabbinical tradition that murder is an evil thing. We would never murder anyone. Therefore, we have kept the law of God 'Thou shalt not kill.' " In fact, the thought that they did not murder was one way in which they convinced themselves they were righteous. (Similarly did they justify themselves with regard to the commandment "Thou shalt not commit adultery" [Ex. 20:14]. Because they didn't commit the overt act of adultery, they convinced themselves that they were holy.) So, if we reject the idea of murder, saying to ourselves, "Why, that terrible breed of humanity— that indescribable vileness that characterizes murderers.

26

They're a different kind of person than I am; I don't murder—I'm not that kind of person," then we are no different
than the Pharisees at that point.

Their religious superficiality is precisely where Jesus wants to
confront the Jews. He has just said, "For I say unto you that
except your righteousness shall exceed the righteousness of
the scribes and Pharisees, ye shall in no case enter into the
kingdom of heaven" (5:20). They were saying, "If we don't
murder, we're righteous." But Jesus said, "Your righteousness
has to exceed that. Not murdering is not enough." And Jesus
gives them a teaching here about murder that is literally
shocking, affecting them in three ways: It affects their view of
themselves, it affects their view of God, and it affects their
view of others. What Jesus is going to say is so dramatic that
it shatters complacent overconfidence.

Lesson

I. THE EFFECT OF JESUS' WORDS UPON THE SELF-RIGH-
TEOUSNESS OF MAN (vv. 21-22)

A. The Tradition of the Jews (v. 21)

"Ye have heard that it was said by them of old, Thou shalt not
kill and whosoever shall kill shall be in danger of judgment."

1. Emphasizing the externals

Jesus was reminding His listeners of the rabbinic tradition
they had been taught; He was not referring to the law of
Moses, though that divine law against killing was reflected in
their teaching. In other words, their tradition on this point
was essentially biblical, having as its foundation Exodus
20:13. But the point that Jesus was making here is that the
rabbinic teaching didn't go far enough. The Jews had taken
God's law and only partially interpreted and applied it so that
they could justify themselves. In fact, the term "judgment"
implies this very thing. It literally meant "the local court." In
other words, Jesus was saying, "Your teaching says you must
not murder, because if you do, you will be in danger of being
punished by the civil court. The problem with that is it
doesn't go far enough." The Jews' full interpretation of the
sixth commandment of the Decalogue was, "Don't kill, because if you do, you will get in trouble with the law." But in
seeking merely to avoid legal problems, the Jews had neglect-
ed God and His holy character. That hadn't even entered into
the discussion. They had made keeping this commandment

so mundane that they didn't even mention God or His divine judgment. Their superficial perspective said nothing about the inner attitudes of the heart.

2. Excluding the internals

However, such an interpretation stopped short of God's intention, as well as His all-seeing eyes. They had forgotten about the rest of the Old Testament, which states that God desires "truth in the inward parts" (Ps. 51:6). Jesus reinforced this truth when He said, "And thou shalt love the Lord thy God with all thy heart, and with all thy soul, and with all thy mind, and with all thy strength. . . . And . . . thy neighbor as thyself" (Mark 12:30*a,* 31*a*). Though the Old Testament clearly taught that God knows the hearts and tries the hearts of men, the Jews had disregarded the internal part of God's law. It wasn't enough for one not to kill; God was concerned about what was going on inside. They had restricted the scope of God's commandment to an earthly court and to an act of murder. That is why they needed to hear:

B. The Teaching of Jesus (v. 22)

"But I say unto you that whosoever is angry with his brother ['without a cause' does not appear in the best manuscripts] shall be in danger of judgment; and whosoever shall say to his brother, Raca, shall be in danger of the council; but whosoever shall say, Thou fool, shall be in danger of hell fire."

1. The indictment by Jesus

Jesus simply says, "It isn't the issue of murder alone; it's the issue of anger and hatred in your heart. You cannot justify yourself because you don't kill, because if there's hatred in your heart, you are the same as a murderer." Jesus' words not only affected the Jews' self-righteousness, but they should affect us, too, as to how we view ourselves. We justify ourselves all the time, admitting that we would never murder, while at the same time we get so angry on the inside with someone that we mock and curse and hold grudges of bitterness.

Implying that God looks at the heart, Jesus swept aside all the rabbinical rubbish and put the emphasis where it belonged—on the attitude. Stripping the Jews of their self-righteousness, He taught that anger is the root of murder and consequently merits equal punishment. Our Lord was saying that what goes on inside of you is what God judges. In terms of the judgment of which you are worthy, you may never kill anyone, but you are just as guilty in God's eyes. In fact, all of us are guilty of this, because even anger with a brother to any degree is the same to God as murder: "Whosoever hateth his brother is a murderer" (1 John 3:15a). Though John had Christians in mind, Jesus used the word "brother" in a broad, generic sense in terms of social relationships. A spiritual brother is not in view, because nobody listening to Jesus at that time would have understood the brotherhood of believers. So, if you have been angry before, whether it has been with Christians or non-Christians, you are a murderer. From God's perspective, there is no difference between your anger and the man who goes out and commits the crime. Jesus strikes hard to show us that even the best of men, if the truth were known, can be the worst of men. You and I sit so smugly, thinking that because we don't commit these kinds of external crimes, we are righteous before God. But Jesus says that if you have ever been angry or have hated, then you are a murderer.

2. The illustrations of judgment

   a) The sin of anger (v. 22a)

   "Whosoever is angry with his brother without a cause shall be in danger of judgment."

   (1) Its exception

   Though anger is a serious sin, there is a righteous anger that we need to talk about, even though that is not what Jesus means here. For example, there was a time when Jesus took a cord and started driving people out of the Temple (John 2:13-17). There are times when God's indignation reaches its absolute limit and explodes in vengeance. There are also times when a believer has a right to be angry. In fact, I believe that the holier we get, the angrier we should be getting about some things. I think we need a little more of this latter kind of anger, especially in a day when everybody wants to talk about love, togetherness, and the absence of conflict. We begin to get so mealymouthed about everything that we won't stand for anything. Some of us ought to learn how to express a little bit of righteous indignation about some of the things that are going on in our country, our churches, and our schools. We also ought to be angry about some of the things our children are exposed to, some of the trends our society is promoting, and some of the things that come waltzing into our homes on television. We ought to have the kind of anger that is not sin: "Be ye angry, and sin not" (Eph. 4:26a). There is a right kind of anger.

(2) Its explanation

However, the anger Jesus is talking about here in verse 22 is selfish anger. "To be angry" in the Greek is *orgizesthai,* and its root is *orgē,* which is sort of a brooding, nursed anger that is not allowed to die—it's a smoldering, longlived kind of thing, for the most part. When you bitterly hold a grudge against somebody, no matter how small, Jesus says that you are as guilty as the person who takes a life, and consequently, you deserve the same judgment. There shouldn't be any difference, because they are both just as serious. In fact, the same Greek word for "judgment" is used at the end of verse 21 to refer to the sentence meted out by a civil court for murder. Likewise, Jesus says, "If you are angry, then you are in danger of execution. Capital punishment should belong to you for anger just as much as for murder." This is a devastating statement, because it forces us to evaluate our attitudes. It isn't a matter of what we do so much as what we are and what we feel. I don't know a civil court in the world that would give the death penalty to somebody for getting angry. But if God is the One sitting on the throne and calling the verdicts, then we had better accept the fact that the one who is angry is as guilty as the one who kills.

b) The sin of slander (v. 22b)

"And whosoever shall say to his brother, Raca, shall be in danger of the council."

Here is another person condemned as a murderer, who ought to go before the council and get the same death penalty. "Raca" is an untranslatable epithet. It was a term of derision that meant something in that time. Consequently, commentators have several ideas about its meaning: "brainless idiot, worthless fellow, silly fool, empty head, blockhead, rock head," and so on. We do know that it was intended as a verbal expression of slander against a person. So our Lord says that contempt is murder committed in the heart, for which the death penalty is equally deserved. What you feel inside is enough to damn you to eternal hell as much as what you do on the outside.

c) The sin of cursing (v. 22c)

"But whosoever shall say, Thou fool [Gk., *mōros*], shall be in danger of hell fire."

(1) Its foolish recipient

Apparently, this was even a worse thing to say to somebody. From a Hebrew perspective, a fool (Gk., *mōros*) was one who rebelled (Heb., *marah,* "to rebel") against God. To accurately call someone a rebel against God would be doing him a favor. But to call him a fool as an epithet of hatred would be a sin. Let me show you the difference:

When Jesus said to the Pharisees, "Ye fools" (Matt. 23:17), it wasn't wrong for Him to say that, because it was true. They were fools who had rebelled against God. The ultimate rebellion is mentioned in Psalm 14:1: "The fool hath said in his heart, There is no God." The fool lives a life of self-will and self-design set against God (Prov. 19:3). You do such a man a favor to tell him, "You're a fool to live like that." Jesus even had to say to some of His own disciples as they were walking on the road to Emmaus, "O foolish ones, and slow of heart to believe" (Luke 24:25a).

(2) Its fiery retribution

By condemning unjustified cursing, Jesus is trying to destroy the religious system of self-righteousness, which can't stand before an examination of the attitudes. Placing before His audience the consequences of such cursing, our Lord gets to the core of the matter. The word He uses for "hell fire" is transliterated from the Greek as *Gehenna.* It is a word with a history and is commonly translated as "hell" (Matt. 5:22, 29, 30; 10:28; 18:9; 23:15, 33; Mark 9:43, 45, 47; Luke 12:5; James 3:6). It is a geographical reference to the Valley of Hinnom on the southwest side of the old city of Jerusalem. Because the valley was historically used as the garbage dump of Jerusalem, where a public incinerator burned continuously, Jesus used it as a vivid illustration to describe the eternal state of hell as an accursed place in which the rubbish of humanity will burn forever. The Valley of Hinnom was a place that had become identified in people's minds as a filthy and accursed place, where useless and evil things were destroyed.

So, Jesus says that even if you are angry and go so far as to speak malicious words and curses against others, then you are as guilty and as liable for eternal hell as a murderer is. In this way Jesus attacks the sin of anger, the sin of slander, and the sin of cursing and with it destroys the scribes' and Pharisees' self-righteousness.

His words have a second effect:

II. THE EFFECT OF JESUS' WORDS UPON THE WORSHIP OF GOD (vv. 23-24)

Jesus now moves from the Pharisees and scribes and other people to Himself as He deals with the area of worship. Worship was a major issue with scribes and Pharisees—their whole life was worship. They were in the Temple all the time supposedly worshiping God—making sacrifices and carrying out the law. Though their life was a circumscribed one of external worship, our Lord here condemns that very worship. Because God is concerned with internal things, such as attitudes toward others, how you feel about your brother, and how you speak to him, Jesus says, "Therefore, if thou bring thy gift to the altar, and there rememberest that thy brother hath anything against thee, leave there thy gift before the altar, and go thy way; first be reconciled to thy brother, and then come and offer thy gift."

A. The Priority of Reconciliation

Jesus says that reconciliation comes before worship. What a powerful point! You are to settle the breach between man and man before you settle the breach between man and God. This shouldn't have been anything new to Jesus' audience, because it had always been God's standard. For example, in Isaiah 1, God said to Israel through Isaiah, "To what purpose is the multitude of your sacrifices unto me? saith the Lord; I am full of the burnt offerings of rams, and the fat of fed beasts, and I delight not in the blood of bullocks, or of lambs, or of hegoats. . . . Bring no more vain oblations; incense is an abomination unto me. . . . Your new moons and your appointed feasts my soul hateth; they are a trouble unto me; I am weary of bearing them. . . . Your hands are full of blood. . . . Learn to do well; seek justice, relieve the oppressed, judge the fatherless, plead for the widow" (vv. 11, 13*a*, 14, 15*b*, 17). He's saying, "Don't you dare come to Me with your religion until you've made your life right with the poor, the oppressed, the orphans, and the widows." In the words of Jesus: "Deal with your brother and then deal with Me. If you Pharisees and scribes come in with all this worship paraphernalia, I don't want any of it. Go away until it's right with your brother."

B. The Perspective of Responsibility

In verse 23, Jesus makes another fascinating point: "Therefore, if thou bring thy gift to the altar, and there rememberest that thy brother hath anything against thee." Did you notice that the issue isn't even your anger, but rather that someone else is angry at you? I do believe, however, the implication here is that the one making the offering has caused the anger of this other one. But whereas verse 22 says that if you're angry, you're in danger of condemnation, verse 23 says that if anybody's angry at you, God doesn't want your worship. Our Lord shows His holiness in the fact that He's not even dealing with the anger of the one worshiping, He is dealing now with the need for resolving the anger against the worshiper. You may know that somebody is upset at you, and even though you may not feel angry toward him, you had better go and settle the issue.

The Worship God Doesn't Want

People who discuss what we can do to improve the quality of worship often miss the point. The way to increase meaningful worship is to get out the people who don't have any business worshiping God because there is something wrong in their personal lives that needs to be resolved. I believe that every Sunday there are husbands and wives who come to church with bitterness between the two of them, and they try to worship God, in spite of the fact that He doesn't want anything to do with hypocritical worship. I believe there are families that attend in which there's animosity from the kids toward the parents or from the parents toward the kids. God isn't interested in their worship. And there are probably others who are internally angry with somebody else in the fellowship or a neighbor on their street. Maybe there's a fellow Christian that we don't particularly care for, and something has happened to cause bitterness. In such cases, the Bible says we are to go away and offer nothing to God, because He is not interested in our worship until the conflict is resolved. Scripture makes this clear. Psalm 66:18 says, "If I regard iniquity in my heart, the Lord will not hear me." First Samuel 15:22 says, "Hath the Lord as great delight in burnt offerings and sacrifices, as in obeying the voice of the Lord? Behold, to obey is better than sacrifice, and to hearken than the fat of rams."

You say, "John, how do I find that person who's angry with me?" Well, I think the implication of the text is that you know this person's angry with you. Obviously there will be people angry with you that you are unaware of, and you can't run around asking everybody. But there are other times when you do know somebody's angry with you. At those times, I try to reconcile with them, and I do my best to make things right, asking their forgiveness. But if they don't forgive me, there's nothing more I can do, and I am free to worship God. Reconciliation with some is a very difficult thing to do. But regardless of that, when I know that reconciliation is needed, Jesus says that it is something that I must try to bring about.

So Jesus' words are devastating, affecting our self-righteousness and how we are to worship Him. Finally, let us examine:

III. THE EFFECT OF JESUS' WORDS UPON RELATIONSHIPS WITH OTHERS (vv. 25-26)

Having already introduced this idea in verses 23 and 24, Jesus now gives a specific example in verses 25 and 26: "Agree with thine adversary quickly, while thou art in the way with him, lest at any time the adversary deliver thee to the judge, and the judge deliver thee to the officer, and thou be cast into prison. Verily I say unto thee, Thou shalt by no means come out from there, till thou hast paid the uttermost farthing." The imagery of our Lord is graphic here. He uses an illustration borrowed from the old legal method of dealing with debtors in Jewish society. The debt of this particular worshiper has come to the place that he is actually being dragged into court over it.

Now the key to the solution is given in verse 25: "Agree with thine adversary quickly." It is the idea of immediately resolving the problem before you continue your worship. Don't just wait until the "right time" for reconciliation to come, because tomorrow may be too late—you may be cast into prison, where you will never be able to pay that debt back. Here our Lord focuses on the guilty party as the one who is worshiping. He is saying, "Settle your case out of court. Don't let this thing continue to the point that reconciliation is impossible." In Jewish law, when a man was adjudged guilty as a debtor, he was handed over to the court officer, who would then try to exact from the individual the payment to the creditor. If he couldn't collect it, the officer would take the man who defaulted and throw him in prison until the debtor paid it back. The point is if you were in prison, you couldn't ever pay it back. Consequently, it was important to reconcile before a severe judgment was determined that would render one unable to reconcile at all.

Now, what does Jesus mean here? Does He mean that the time will come when the person will die and you'll never be able to reconcile, or does He mean that the time will come when God will chasten you and it will be too late? Possibly He means both of those things. The main point is simply that we can't worship Him unless our relationships with others are right, so hurry and make them right—don't let them go to the place where there will be a civil judgment made and somebody loses in the end. Don't let it go too far. Don't let it go to the place where God, in judgment, moves in. Act before then. I believe, in the final analysis, Jesus is saying that God is the real judge and hell is the real punishment. And if you don't make things right, you may find yourself in an eternal hell with a debt that could never be paid.

Conclusion

At this point, a summarization might be helpful for better understanding. Jesus has been saying, in effect, "You Pharisees and scribes who are depending on your own self-righteousness think you are holy just because you don't kill. But let Me tell you something: If you're angry, if you've ever said a malicious word about somebody's character, if you've ever cursed anybody—you are like a murderer. If you have ever come to worship God and had something against your brother, you are in danger of judgment for such hypocrisy. You are obligated to postpone your worship and to immediately seek reconciliation. The fact that you don't murder is a little piece of the iceberg. If you have grudges that you've never settled, you worship in hypocrisy. If you curse, malign, and are angry, the same judgment comes upon you for that—death and hell are what you deserve." And thus does Jesus speak to the issues of self-righteousness, of worship, and of relationships with others. He devastates the comfort of the scribes and Pharisees regarding their assumed self-righteousness by setting a standard so high that nobody can keep it.

Who is a murderer? Have you ever been angry or called anybody a name, whether a family member or a stranger? Have you ever cursed anybody? Have you ever come to church to worship while you had bitterness in your heart? Have you ever had a legal conflict with somebody that dragged out all the way to the court and was never settled? Then you are the same as a murderer, because you allowed bitterness, hatred, and anger to enter your heart.

Let me ask a second question: Who deserves death and hell? You do, and I do—we're all guilty of murder. We have all sinned and come short of the glory of God (Rom. 3:23), and the wages of sin is death (Rom. 6:23a). But you say, "Well, how do we escape? If we're all murderers and no murderer will inherit the kingdom, because he is deserving of death and hell, then how do we escape? After all, everyone at one time or

35

another has worshiped in hypocrisy, been angry, said malicious things, thought or spoken a curse, been unreconciled to a brother—we've all done those things. What are we going to do?" This is the question that Jesus hopes His audience will ask. He wants to drive His listeners to the fact that they cannot be righteous on their own, which ought to bring them to their knees for the righteousness that only He can give. Everything that He says here is to drive them to frustration and inadequacy so that they come to Him.

We too must realize that He died our death and entered our hell that we might have righteousness. You and I both deserve death, because we not only are murderers, but we have committed numerous other crimes as well. However, Jesus offers us the gift of His own righteousness—that's the meaning of the gospel. This righteousness that we desperately need comes only as a gift from God, for "by the deeds of the law there shall no flesh be justified" (Rom. 3:20*a*). It is the righteousness of Jesus Christ that is imputed to us (Rom. 4:6; 2 Cor. 5:21).

God had every reason to be angry with us, didn't He? God had every reason to hold us in contempt and to righteously curse us, because we were murderers. But even though we were as foul as the Mansons, or the Coronas, or any of the other slashers and slayers of this world (in terms of our un-Christlike attitudes), He loves and forgives us, having paid our debt. And the wonder of wonders is that He seeks to reconcile us to Himself in His eternal kingdom, because He wants to have fellowship with us! Isn't that incredible? If such an absolutely holy God can so desire to be reconciled to vile murderers like us, can we follow the pattern of His Son and find it in our hearts to be reconciled to our brothers?

Focusing on the Facts

1. What did God institute as the consequential penalty for murder (see p. 24)?
2. What types of killing does Exodus 20:13 not have in mind (see pp. 24-25)?
3. What are a few things that the Bible says about murder (see pp. 25-26)?
4. Though the rabbinic tradition regarding murder was basically biblical, what was Jesus' criticism about it (see p. 27)?
5. What had the Jews done with God's law so that they could justify themselves (see p. 27)?
6. What Old Testament truth did Jesus reinforce in Mark 12:30-31 (see p. 28)?
7. To what had the Jews restricted the scope of God's commandment (see p. 28)?

8. What did Jesus teach was the root of murder, that merits equal punishment (see p. 28)?
9. What type of anger are we justified in having? What is the type of anger that Jesus was condemning (see p. 29)?
10. In the Old Testament, what was one called who rebelled against God (see p. 31)?
11. When is it a sin to call someone a fool, and when is it a favor (see p. 31)?
12. Why was the Valley of Hinnom used to refer to hell (see p. 31)?
13. In Matthew 5:23, what does Jesus say must come before worship (see p. 32)?
14. In verse 22, the one with anger is condemned, whereas in verse 23, the one who is the object of anger is under divine obligation to resolve the problem. What attribute of God does this emphasize? Explain (see p. 33).
15. Though reconciliation can be a difficult thing to do, when must you try to bring it about? If a person refuses to forgive you, why would you then still be free to worship God (see pp. 33-34)?
16. What is the key in Matthew 5:25 that tells how we should resolve our problems? Why is this important (see p. 34)?
17. According to Jesus' teaching, who is a murderer (see p. 35)?
18. If we are all murderers, what is the only way we can be righteous in God's eyes (see pp. 35-36)?

Pondering the Principles

1. Take a moment to think about the reasons that you attend church, participate on church committees, read the Bible, pray, and do other Christian activities. Is there any reservation in your heart that you are doing them to serve God out of love? Do external consequences alone determine the direction of your spiritual life, such as worrying about what others will think if you don't do this or that? Is your behavior just biblical enough to get by the scrutiny of the human eye? Because God desires "truth in the inward parts" (Ps. 51:6), establish the positive habit of always viewing everything you think, do, and say from the perspective of God and His holiness. Continually ask yourself, "What does God feel about this?"
2. Have you ever had any righteous anger about something that was a corruption of God's moral standards and was in direct contradiction to biblical principles? Did you take action, or did you procrastinate and rationalize that it wasn't important and that somebody else would take care of it? There once was a news story about a residential building burning down during rush-hour traffic and killing those inside, because no one called the fire department soon enough. Evidently, people thought somebody else would report it. Therefore,

don't become apathetic about something you initially thought was important, especially if it opposes biblical truths and principles. List some of the things that directly or indirectly affect your life that you believe you need to take a stand against. What are some steps you can take to effectively confront those things?

3. Do you know of anyone with whom you are angry? Do you know of anyone who is angry with you? Determine to set that relationship aright, even if you are not at fault. Pray that God would grant you the boldness to initiate the reconciliation, the mercy and humility to forgive, and the love to bind any emotional wounds.

4. Compare 1 Samuel 15:22 with Romans 12:1. What type of sacrifice is God primarily interested in? How would you best describe the type of sacrifice you are giving: a performance of the approved religious practices with the wrong attitudes or a life of obedient service to your Lord? For some ideas on how you can sacrificially give yourself in service to God, read the rest of Romans 12.

5. Jesus paid our debt of obedience and holiness, which was infinitely beyond our ability to repay. After meditating upon Colossians 1:19-23, take some time to praise God for loving and forgiving us far above what we ever will deserve.

3

Who Is an Adulterer?—Part 1

Outline

Introduction
A. The Teaching of Our Savior
  1. Reestablishing the standard
  2. Rebuking the self-righteous
    a) The proclamation of the illustration
    b) The purpose of the illustration
    c) The power of the illustration
B. The Trends of Our Society
  1. The evaluation of its sexual preoccupation
  2. The evaluation from a scriptural perspective
    a) The perversions of sex condemned (1 Cor. 6:13-18)
      (1) The explanation of Paul
      (2) The effects of perversion
    b) The purpose of sex confirmed (1 Cor. 7:3-5)

Lesson
 I. The Standard of God's Law
   A. Lowered by the Jews
   B. Lifted Back Up by Jesus
 II. The Summary of God's Law
   A. Expressed in Deuteronomy
    1. The relationship of love
      a) Emphasized
      b) Explained
    2. The response to love
      a) Stated
      b) Supported
      c) Surveyed
        (1) The application
        (2) The affirmation
        (3) The alternatives
        (4) The appeal
   B. Expressed in the Decalogue
    1. Its purpose

Introduction

A. The Teaching of Our Savior

In the fifth chapter of Matthew, our Lord answers the question in the forefront of the minds of the people who had seen His miracles and heard His teaching: "Was this miracle worker the Messiah who would bring God's kingdom?" There were certain elements in the teaching and ministry of Jesus that made them think He might be the One. They also wanted to know what the standards were for His kingdom, and whether or not they conformed to the law of God and the teaching of Moses. Therefore, Jesus summarizes His message to them in Matthew 5:17-20 with the following words: "Think not that I am come to destroy the law, or the prophets; I am not come to destroy, but to fulfill. For verily I say unto you, Till heaven and earth pass, one jot or one tittle shall in no way pass from the law, till all be fulfilled. Whosoever, therefore, shall break one of these least commandments, and shall teach men so, he shall be called the least in the kingdom of heaven; but whosoever shall do and teach them, the same shall be called great in the kingdom of heaven. For I say unto you that except your righteousness shall exceed the righteousness of the scribes and Pharisees, ye shall in no case enter into the kingdom of heaven." In other words, He was saying, "I am the Messiah, and My message is the same message that Moses gave you—not any different. I will not change or destroy it, because I came to fulfill it. However, the standards for My kingdom must exceed the standards that you are now living by."

1. Reestablishing the standard

Now, there was the basic standard that Jesus gave. He required a righteousness beyond that of the scribes and Pharisees, who supposedly were the most righteous people in the Jewish society. Jesus was demanding more than they asked, but not more than Moses asked. The standard of the law demanded more than even the most seemingly righteous Jews were giving. Consequently, this was a difficult statement for the Jews to understand. It did not make sense to them that He could accept the law and still require a higher righteousness than that of the scribes and Pharisees, who appeared as though they lived the law of Moses to the hilt. For this reason, the question in the minds of the people was, "If You believe in the law of Moses, how can You require a greater standard than the scribes and Pharisees who teach us that law?"

Though the scribes and the Pharisees sat in the seat of Moses, claiming to be the proponents of the law of Moses, in reality, they themselves had lowered the law of Moses to their own design and, as a result, were not even keeping that which God originally intended. This is why Jesus comes to lift the standard back to where it was in the beginning. In doing this, Jesus gives His listeners several illustrations of how the religious leaders and the people fell short on every aspect of God's absolute standard. He wants them to see that the people were not living up to God's standard, which they had lowered, and so He must raise it back to where it really should be. In effect, what He does here is to destroy any system of self-righteousness.

God, Created in the Image of Man

What man tends to do is this: If he doesn't want to come God's way, he creates his own god as well as a compatible religious system so that he can say, "This is what is required. Therefore, this is what I'll accomplish so that I can be justified." Man drags the law of God down to something he can do, does it, and then convinces himself he's OK. A typical response today to the question, "What are you going to do when you die?" would be, "Well, I hope I'm going to heaven on the basis that I am a pretty good guy. God certainly will take me to heaven." In other words, man invents the kind of god he wants with the kind of standards he can keep so he can consider himself righteous. But what we can say to a person like that today is, "That's not the way it is. The standard of God is too high—you can't keep it." This is exactly what Jesus said.

2. Rebuking the self-righteous

The scribes and the Pharisees invented a standard lower than the divine one, figured out how they could keep it, and kept it the best they could, convincing themselves they were righteous. But Jesus says, "Not on your life! Unless your righteousness exceeds that of the scribes and the Pharisees, you'll never enter into My kingdom. Rather than violating the law of Moses, in terms of adding to it or changing it, I am simply reiterating where Moses put it in the beginning. Let's get it back where it belongs!" So Jesus reestablishes God's original standard so that He might destroy the people's false sense of security in their own self-righteousness. Contrasting the righteousness they thought they had with the true, divine standard, He literally strips all men and women stark naked, spiritually speaking, before God, until they realize that they have no claim of self-righteousness left. Let's see how He does this by briefly looking at the illustration in verses 27 to 30:

a) The proclamation of the illustration

"Ye have heard that it was said by them of old, Thou shalt not commit adultery; But I say unto you that whosoever looketh on a woman to lust after her hath committed adultery with her already in his heart" (vv. 27-28). In other words, Jesus is saying, "Your tradition taught to you by the scribes and Pharisees says that if you just don't commit adultery, you are righteous. But that standard is too low—let's put it back where God intended it. God never was solely concerned about the act, but rather primarily the attitude behind it."

Then, in verse 29-30, Jesus gives them a hyperbolic solution for meeting the divine standard: "And if thy right eye offends thee, pluck it out, and cast it from thee; for it is profitable for thee that one of thy members should perish, and not that thy whole body should be cast into hell. And if thy right hand offend thee, cut it off, and cast it from thee; for it is profitable for thee that one of thy members should perish, and not that thy whole body should be cast into hell." In other words, you are a lot better off to cut off your arm or to pluck out your eye if it leads you to sin, which includes not simply what you do, but also what you feel and think in your heart.

b) The purpose of the illustration

With this second illustration of adultery, Jesus is confronting the self-righteous, saying, "You can't say that because you didn't actually carry out the sin that you are all right, for if you ever thought it, you have committed it in God's eyes. If you ever lusted, desiring to commit this sin, then you are a sinner who cannot claim to be righteous. It is no different than if you were angry with your brother. Even though you didn't actually murder him, you still would be guilty."

Now, whereas His illustration in verses 21-22 dealt with the sixth commandment, the illustration in verses 27-28 deals with the seventh commandment, their underlying principles being the sacredness of life, and the sacredness of marriage, respectively. Using these two illustrations, Jesus says, "You are not righteous before God if you've ever been angry or if you've ever thought of committing adultery." He is trying to show them how really sinful they are, no matter what their outside behavior may be.

c) The power of the illustration

Anger and sex are two very powerful elements that really reach deep down into human experience. They aptly illustrate the sinfulness of man, cutting to the very core of the issue. We've all experienced the common temptations of anger and lust, which reach deep into the basic sinfulness of man. And those Jews who were sitting on the hillside in Galilee hearing the Lord Jesus Christ confront them about the anger and lust in their hearts would have to admit by virtue of their own consciences that they were indeed sinners. The fact that they never killed anybody or committed the act of adultery didn't exonerate them from the sinfulness which reigned in their hearts. Jesus wants to go right to the heart of man and show them that no matter what they have or haven't done, they can't fit into His kingdom, thereby exhibiting God's unattainable standard.

Are sexual temptations worse in our society?

The fact that Jesus says anybody who looks on a woman to lust after her has committed adultery with her already in his heart is a tremendous statement to somebody living in our society today, when the temptations are so vast. Temptation has always been around—it didn't matter whether a woman was covered from head to foot in a long robe and a veil, the temptation would still be there. There have always been those things that the devil would use to generate lust and that the flesh would pounce upon to initiate the temptation. However, it seems to me that in the virtueless society in which we live, the temptations are so much more rampant and so much more visible.

B. The Trends of Our Society

1. The evaluation of its sexual preoccupation

I believe that sex in marriage, in the beauty of which God has designed it, was meant to be a very personal discovery—not something plastered all over billboards and taught in classes and presented in books. I think it's something very private, special, and unique. The fact that we incessantly teach and talk about sex only serves to elicit evil responses out of the hearts of evil men and evil women. It doesn't do anything to help the situation. For example, we find explicit sex seminars and books everywhere. There are people constantly preaching on the subject, advocating this and that. I have even heard the strangest kind of counseling coming from men of God. I heard one man who is a minister saying that couples ought to take a shower together before they get married so that they will know what they're getting into. That kind of counsel is just exactly the thing that Jesus said is wrong and is nothing more than a manifestation of sinfulness. I don't think ever in the history of the western world since the death of Greek and Roman paganism have we seen the unbridled indulgence of sexual passion so encouraged and so elicited and so praised as we do today.

It won't be long until you're going to have to take your television and put your foot through it. Mass media lures with sex to sell its products and glamorizes illicit pleasure. Sex crimes are at an all-time high. Divorce, infidelity, and perversion are being praised and are subjects for humor in our society. The "pleasure first" philosophy of hedonism is rampant and in full force. Monogamous marriage is threatened, and marital fidelity is ridiculed and mocked. We could cite numerous examples of the decline of morality in our society, but that is not necessary, because you can clearly see its effects all around you. I even have to avoid looking at magazine racks, because I don't want to bombard my mind with what is there on some of the covers, let alone on the inside.

44

A new morality of situation ethics has been espoused, which basically says that right is relative and you ought to do whatever feels good as long as it doesn't hurt anybody else. Our whole society is so preoccupied with sex that it's beyond belief. An illustration by C. S. Lewis shows how ludicrous it is: He says that you can get a large audience together for a strip-tease act—that is, to watch a girl undress on a stage. And if that doesn't indicate how warped our view of sex and womanhood is, imagine going to a country where you could fill a theater by bringing in a covered plate on the stage and then slowly lifting the cover to let everyone see, just before the lights went out, that it contained a mutton chop or a piece of bacon. Wouldn't you think that something had gone wrong with their appetite for food? Should we not think that it's just as ridiculous for our society to be so infatuated with somebody taking off her clothes? The Playboy philosophy is nothing but a mutton chop mentality—it's a perversion. Hugh Hefner comes along and says that we shouldn't get all upset about sex, because it's only "a biological necessity like eating, drinking and sleeping." That kind of philosophy is not new, though. It comes right out of Greek and Roman paganism.

2. The evaluation from a scriptural perspective

   a) The perversions of sex condemned (1 Cor. 6:13-18)

      (1) The explanation of Paul

         The apostle Paul reiterates that ancient philosophy as he confronts the Corinthians about their preoccupation with the wrong perspective of sex. Essentially, they were saying, "Foods for the body, and the body for foods" (v. 13*a*). In other words, the Corinthians used this proverbial response to prove that sex is only a biological thing like eating, sleeping, or drinking. However, Paul responds to their indifference, saying, "But God shall destroy both it and them. Now the body is not for fornication, but for the Lord; and the Lord for the body" (v. 13). Because the body belongs to God, you can't just give it over to indulgence and say, "It's only biology." That's the mutton chop philosophy. Continuing his rebuke, Paul says, "Know ye not that your bodies are the members of Christ? Shall I, then, take the members of Christ, and make them the members of an harlot? God forbid. What? Know ye not that he who is joined to an harlot is one body? . . . But he that is joined unto the Lord is one spirit" (vv.

45

15-16*a,* 17). In other words, if you enter into an adulterous situation, you join the Lord to that sin. There are spiritual implications with what the Christian does with his body. This is why Paul so adamantly says in verse 18, "Flee fornication [Gk., *porneia,* 'evil sexual behavior']."

(2) The effects of perversion

The view that sex is only a biological urge and you need to live it up and enjoy the present regardless of the consequences is the logcial result of situation ethics: "Don't be restrained and inhibited—live it up with whomever you want. It's just biology anyway." That philosophy is drowning our society in a sea of sexual perversion. It has bombarded us with a barrage of propaganda that is shattering families and ruining individual lives by destroying the capability of an individual to do what is right unless he has completely committed himself to Jesus Christ. Relationships have been replaced with perversions, concern with concupiscence, and love with lechery. That's the way it is in our society.

On the other hand, whenever you talk about sex, you not only have the people who sit up in their chair because it's their favorite subject, you also have the people who grab their Bibles and head for the door. The latter are considered rather prudish because they hold the Victorian view, which goes to the opposite extreme, saying that sex is shameful and less than holy. Such a reactionary view has been practiced in the present as well as in the past. But that's not the answer either. You can't go to the extreme of saying that sex is purely a biological function, and you can't go to the other extreme and say that castration will solve the problem. One is just as much a perversion as the other, because God has wonderfully designed sex as a part of human life.

b) The purpose of sex confirmed (1 Cor. 7:3-5)

The apostle Paul discusses God's design of a physical relationship, saying, "Let the husband render unto the wife her due; and likewise also, the wife unto the husband. The wife hath not power of her own body, but the husband; and likewise also the husband hath not power of his own body, but the wife. Defraud ye not [or 'stop depriving'] one the other, except it be with consent for a time, that ye may give yourselves to fasting and prayer; and come together again, that Satan tempt you not for your incontinency [or 'lack of self-control']." In other words, he says that you have every right and responsibility to give your body to your husband and wife in the fulfillment of sexual desire.

God has designed the physical relationship and has sanctified and blessed it, as is apparent from the Song of Solomon, which describes the beauty of human love in a marital situation. So it is that sex is pure and right, but our world has made a mutton chop mentality out of it. It has been degenerated into a twisted, jaded, and lecherous perversion that appeals to the hearts of sinful, evil men.

Now, as we come to this passage in Matthew 5:27-32, we need to recognize that it is a very fitting word for the society in which we live. Let us discover what it is teaching.

Lesson

I. THE STANDARD OF GOD'S LAW

A. Lowered by the Jews

Now the Pharisees had their own viewpoint about not committing adultery. They felt that because they didn't do it they were righteous; they thought they'd go right into the kingdom and have the chief seats. Maybe you're like that. Maybe you say to yourself, "I'm not so bad. I've never actually gone out on my wife and committed adultery." But Jesus says if you ever look on a woman to lust after her you've done it in your heart, and that's enough to damn you to hell forever. That is the implication of verses 29-30. Your self-confidence is shattered here, because the external system of law is unable to meet God's standard, which takes your attitude into account.

Jesus wants to show His listeners that they can't help themselves, in spite of the fact that they can control their actions. They could avoid committing adultery, but they couldn't do anything with the inside that they were essentially powerless to change. This realization should have driven them in desperation to seek God, who alone can change the heart. They desperately wanted to believe they were OK, but Jesus shows them they weren't.

Now, because the standard of God's law had been lowered by the Jews, it had to be:

47

B. Lifted Back Up by Jesus

Notice the contrast between the beginnings of verses 27 and 28: "Ye have heard . . . but I say. . . ." This same formula is used in verses 21 and 22, 31 and 32, 33 and 34, 38 and 39, and 43 and 44. It points to the Jews' misunderstanding of God's law, which Jesus addressed in this fashion: "You have heard from the rabbis, who interpreted the law; but I'm telling you the truth of the law—the standard you have is not right, nor is it sufficient. Your teachers of tradition have reduced the law of God to a simple external, and, consequently, they haven't given you the whole story. They have told you that if you don't commit adultery, then you're OK; but I'm telling you there's more to this than just that. You have merely invented a system that you can live up to and then convinced yourself that you are righteous."

The self-righteous who were listening to Jesus teach could avoid committing adultery, but they couldn't do anything about their secret life. They had missed the whole point of the Old Testament, where God had said, "Thou shalt not commit adultery" (Ex. 20:14). And when God gave any other precept in the Old Testament, He was talking about far more than the deed itself, which is what Jesus wants them to understand. Let me show you what I mean by discussing:

II. THE SUMMARY OF GOD'S LAW

The basic revelation of God's message to man came through Moses in the form of the Pentateuch, which essentially is the core of the Old Testament. The prophets and the writings that follow the Mosaic writings are simply explanations, commentaries, or elaborations of what is contained in the law of Moses. Many times as you read through the prophets, you find the various prophets indicting the people because they had failed to keep the law of Moses. It is the Pentateuch that sets the pace and contains, as it were, the gospel of God given through Moses. The rest of the Old Testament elaborates on that law of God laid down through Moses. God revealed His basic requirements through Moses, elaborated on them in the prophets and the writings, and consummated them in Jesus Christ, who came not to change anything, but to clear up the issue that the law of Moses hadn't changed.

Now, the essence of the law of Moses is:

A. Expressed in Deuteronomy

In Deuteronomy, the fifth and last of the five books of Moses, we have a summary of the law of God. I believe that Deuteronomy is the most important book in the Old Testament. It was the reiteration of the law (hence, its Greek name which means "second law") given by God to Israel as the nation was about to enter and take possession of the land He had promised them. It served as a summarization of all the standards for living in God's kingdom. The centrality of the book of Deuteronomy is supported by the facts that the Ten Commandments are repeated in the fifth chapter and that Jesus and the New Testament writers quoted this book more than any other from the Old Testament. This critical book is the summarization of the entire Old Testament, because essentially all that follows it comments upon the Pentateuch, of which Deuteronomy is the key. In fact, I believe that a summary of the entire Bible is contained in Deuteronomy, which stresses the importance of:

1. The relationship of love

  a) Emphasized

   Deuteronomy 6:5 says, "And thou shalt love the Lord thy God with all thine heart, and with all thy soul, and with all thy might." That principle, which is the pinnacle of the whole Bible, is complemented with a secondary principle also conveyed in Deuteronomy, though more explicitly stated in Leviticus 19:18: "Thou shalt love thy neighbor as thyself." Now there you have the consummation of all of God's truth. Jesus verified this when He said, "Thou shalt love the Lord, thy God, with all thy heart, and with all thy soul, and with all thy mind. This is the first and great commandment. And the second is like it, Thou shalt love thy neighbor as thyself. On these two commandments hang all the law and the prophets" (Matt. 22:37-40).

  b) Explained

   The Old Testament is not building a relationship on law, it is building a relationship on love. So many people do not understand that. They think the Old Testament economy was an economy of law—it wasn't. It was an economy of love. It is a relationship that God is after. Love is the key to a relationship with God, which is made clear all throughout Deuteronomy, where God continues to say, "I want you to love Me. I want a wholehearted commitment of true devotion."

Besides the relationship of a man to God, Deuteronomy also stresses:

2. The response to love

  a) Stated

   Throughout Deuteronomy, Moses says to Israel over and over again as they prepare to enter the land, "You must love the Lord, because it is a relationship of love that God has always sought with man." Before God ever gave the law to Israel in the form of the Ten Commandments and all the other statutes and regulations, He established a relationship with them. He first loved Israel, delivering them out of Egypt. It was only after establishing a loving relationship with them and accomplishing redemption that He gave them the law. Therefore, the law was not the cause of the relationship, it was the result of it. In other words, God first freed Israel from Egypt, made them His people, and after that, said, "This is how you are to live."

b) Supported

The New Testament confirms these words of Moses, whether it is Jesus, Paul, Peter, James, or John who is speaking. For example, John said, "We love him, because he first loved us" (1 John 4:19). God loved Israel—that's how it all began. Similarly, we were first brought into a relationship of love with God, and then we had a response of obedience to His law. It is the attitude that God has always been after. It is not that God wanted them to keep a bunch of external laws, it is that He wanted them to be self-motivated to love Him. That's why Jesus says, "It isn't an issue of whether you don't murder or commit adultery. The issue is what is in your heart." It's always been that way.

This isn't anything unique to the New Testament, as Deuteronomy 10 shows. Rather than starting with the requirement to keep the Ten Commandments, notice what Moses says: "And now, Israel, what doth the Lord thy God require of thee, but to fear the Lord thy God, to walk in all his ways, and to love him, and to serve the Lord thy God with all thy heart and with all thy soul, [and then] to keep the commandments of the Lord, and his statutes, which I command thee this day for thy good?" (vv. 12-13). That's no different than what the New Testament teaches when it says that if you profess to know and love God and yet you don't keep His commandments, you are a liar (1 John 2:4). The love comes first, and then the obedience.

Deuteronomy 10 even sets forth the second dimension, that of loving one's neighbor, which finds its source in loving God first: "Love ye, therefore, the sojourner; for ye were sojourners in the land of Egypt. Thou shalt fear the Lord thy God; him shalt thou serve, and to him shalt thou cleave. . . . Therefore, thou shalt love the Lord thy God, and keep his charge, and his statutes, and his ordinances, and his commandments, always" (10:19-20*a;* 11:1). Can you see that it is the reciprocating love of a heart relationship that God desires from man? This is why Moses says in 10:16, "Circumcise, therefore, the foreskin of your heart." God has always sought the attitude of the heart. Never has He been satisfied with merely an external response. This is evident from the main theme of the first eleven chapters of Deuteronomy, which can be summarized in the statement, "Love God, and love your neighbor." That's what God requires of you, and it is exactly what Jesus and the epistles repeat in the New Testament.

c) Surveyed

   (1) The application

   Then, in Deuteronomy 12-25, Moses interprets and applies these two basic principles of loving God and loving your neighbor to every daily situation, giving them various statutes which implement these principles.

   (2) The affirmation

   When it comes to chapter 26, he gathers everybody together for a service of dedication, where the people confess their sins and rededicate their lives as an affirmation of their love for God. It is a time for their hearts to be committed to the Lord and a time of great praise and worship as Moses challenges them to serve God from their hearts in obedience: "This day the Lord thy God hath commanded thee to do these statutes and ordinances; thou shalt, therefore, keep and do them with all thine heart, and with all thy soul" (v. 16). In chapter 27, Moses tells them, "Joshua is going to take you into the land, because I have forfeited that privilege. And when you get there, the first thing I want you to do is renew this same commitment that you will love the Lord and each other."

   (3) The alternatives

   Then, in chapter 28, he says to them, "Now you have two choices: You can be blessed or you can be cursed." He delineates the blessings in verses 3-13, and the curses throughout the rest of the chapter. In other words, he is saying, "When you get into the land, if you choose to love the Lord your God with all your heart, and to love your neighbor, you will be blessed.

But if you choose not to love the Lord and your neighbor, you will be cursed."

(4) The appeal

In chapters 29-30, Moses appeals to the people to make a decision about what they will do: "For this commandment which I command thee this day, it is not hidden from thee, neither is it far off. It is not in heaven, that thou shouldest say, Who shall go up for us to heaven, and bring it unto us, that we may hear it, and do it? Neither is it beyond the sea, that thou shouldest say, Who shall go over the sea for us, and bring it unto us, that we may hear it, and do it? But the word is very near unto thee, in thy mouth, and in thy heart, that thou mayest do it" (30:11-14). In other words, "You have a choice to make, and the information is sufficient to make a wise decision. You can choose blessing for loving God with all your heart and your neighbor as yourself, or you can choose cursing for not doing that. But don't complain that you didn't have the information, because it's available here."

"See, I have set before thee this day life and good, and death and evil, in that I command thee this day to love the Lord thy God, to walk in his ways, and to keep his commandments and his statutes and his ordinances, that thou mayest live and multiply; and the Lord thy God shall bless thee in the land to which thou goest to possess it. But if thine heart turn away, so that thou wilt not hear, but shalt be drawn away, and worship other gods, and serve them, I declare unto you this day, that ye shall surely perish, and that ye shall not prolong your days upon the land, to which thou passest over the Jordan to go to possess it. I call heaven and earth to record this day against you, that I have set before you life and death, blessing and cursing; therefore, choose life, that both thou and thy seed may live, that thou mayest love the Lord thy God, and that thou mayest obey his voice, and that thou mayest cleave unto him; for he is thy life, and the length of thy days; that thou mayest dwell in the land which the Lord swore unto thy fathers, to Abraham, to Isaac, and to Jacob, to give them" (vv. 15-20).

So this is the sum of the whole Old Testament: love God. God has always wanted a heart relationship. He didn't approve of anyone in the Old Testament who just mechanically kept the

Ten Commandments. That didn't fulfill the plan of God. The Ten Commandments were only given to regulate a relationship that was based on love, and if the love relationship wasn't there, the regulation didn't mean anything. That's the point. The centrality of God's concern is the heart, not the externals. Though the Pharisees were satisfied with the externals, they had really missed the point, which is the reason Jesus said, "Ye have heard that it was said . . . but I say unto you . . ." In other words, "You're preoccupied with the outside, and God is concerned with the inside." It is a relationship of love that God wants, and the law only regulates it, just as the standards of the New Testament regulate a New Covenant relationship with the Lord.

When you come to Matthew 22:34-40, you find our Lord reiterating the same thing that comes out of Deuteronomy, which He identifies as the two greatest commandments. He says, in effect, "I don't care what your functions are or what performances you make; if you don't love God and your neighbor, you've missed the point." That's why Jesus could say to the rich young ruler, "It's wonderful that you've kept all the commandments from your youth, but you know what you haven't done? You haven't manifested a right heart attitude, because you haven't demonstrated your love for your neighbor by being willing to sell all you have and giving it to the poor." This merely betrayed the fact that while there was an external behavior, there was nothing going on inside. It was hypocritical.

The Final Fulfillment for the Frustration and Futility Through Failure

1. The purpose of the standard

   There is a reason for love being God's internal standard that no one can keep. In the Old Testament, God established this standard: "Love the Lord your God with all your heart, soul, mind and strength, and love your neighbor as yourself." But the people in the Old Testament would admit that they were unable to keep God's standard, which is exactly what God wanted them to recognize. When they couldn't keep it, they experienced the guilt of sin. However, God didn't just leave them helpless and frustrated in their conviction; He gave them the sacrificial system to deal with their inability to keep His perfect standard. When a man or a woman admitted, "I can't keep the law of God, and I'm overwhelmed with my sin," God said, "Then confess your sin to Me and prove the genuineness of that confession by an act of sacrifice." The sacrificial system didn't make men right with God; it simply pointed out that only God could make them right with Him. It pointed out they needed a sacrifice, because of their inability to keep God's standard regarding a relationship of love. When men couldn't fulfill all that the standard required, they became guilty and convicted of sin. But in order to deal with guilt, God provided a sacrificial system, which, in and of itself, never gave a lasting peace and relief from guilt. Yet, in its futility, the system pointed to the fact that someday, someplace, in some way, there had to be an ultimate sacrifice that would do away with sin once and for all.

2. The provision of a Savior

The whole sacrificial system pointed to Jesus Christ. Therefore, the gospel of Moses was the gospel of Christ. Moses had presented a standard of a loving relationship that a man in his evil heart couldn't fulfill. But even making a sacrifice out of contrition was futile, because the process never ended nor fully accomplished complete forgiveness. It pointed to Jesus Christ as the final sacrifice and fruition of everything Moses ever taught. The whole sequence pointed to the Savior, because He is the only One who could deal with man on the inside.

The Old Testament sacrificial system served to frustrate man, to show him his desperation, and to show him that he couldn't save himself no matter what he did. If the heart relationship wasn't right, he wasn't right.

So, by the time you get to Jesus' day, the Jews had lowered the standard, disregarding the necessity of having a heart relationship. The very fact that they asked Him what the greatest commandment was implies they had forgotten what God's internal standard requires: "Hear, O Israel: The Lord our God is one Lord; and thou shalt love the Lord thy God" (Mark 12:29b-30a). For centuries the standard had slipped by their own choice. They had done away with the part they couldn't keep and stuck with the externals.

Furthermore, the summary of God's internal law was:

B. Expressed in the Decalogue

1. Its purpose

Now you ask, "How do the Ten Commandments fit in?" That's easy. The Ten Commandments were simply a way to regulate love, that's all. Did you know the Ten Commandments are just a definition of love? You say, "I've heard the Ten Commandments are law: 'Thou shalt not do this or that.'" No, they are simply a way to regulate the expression of love. First of all, redemption preceded the giving of the Ten Commandments: Israel was first called out of Egypt and redeemed and ordained as God's people. Then, after God had set His affection upon them, came the code of ethics. Once the relationship was established, the principles of behavior were laid out. But never forget it—redemption preceded law, because God is always concerned with relationship. The relationship preceded the law or the Ten Commandments. The law did not establish the covenant—love established the covenant. The law merely regulated behavior within that covenant.

2. Its particulars

So, the Ten Commandments are essentially nothing more than instructions about how to love God and how to love your neighbor. Did you know that the first four commandments relate to our love for God, and the last six commandments relate to our love for our neighbor? In Exodus 20, we find the initial listing of the Ten Commandments:

a) Affecting our relationship with God

(1) Love is loyal (v. 3)

"Thou shalt have no other gods before me."

If I say to my wife, "Honey, I love you," and then I tell her I also have three of four others that I love too, she is not going to be interested in that kind of love. Loving God means loyally worshiping Him alone. You don't say, "Oh boy, I am really mad. I only have one God and everybody else in the world gets a whole bunch!" No, there are some people who worship one God because they feel that they are right in doing it. There are others who worship one God because they love Him so much. I don't worship the Lord just because I'm trying to fulfill some legal obligation. I worship the one God because He's the only One I love.

(2) Love is faithful (vv. 4-6)

"Thou shalt not make unto thee any carved image, or any likeness of anything that is in heaven above, or that is in the earth beneath, or that is in the water under the earth; thou shalt not bow down thyself to them, nor serve them; for I, the Lord thy God, am a jealous God, visiting the iniquity of the fathers upon the children unto the third and fourth generation of them that hate me; and showing mercy unto thousands of them that love me, and keep my commandments."

Do you see it there? Again it's love. In other words, the point is that love will be faithful, love will not make a carved replica of some nonexistent god. Love is loyal, and its loyalty extends into the future and thus becomes faithfulness. If we love the Lord our God with all our heart, soul, mind, and strength, we'll love only Him, and we'll love Him faithfully.

Third, the next commandment teaches that:

(3) Love is reverent (v. 7)

"Thou shalt not take the name of the Lord thy God in vain; for the Lord will not hold him guiltless that taketh his name in vain."

If you love the Lord your God with all your heart, soul, mind, and strength, would you curse His name? No, because love is reverent.

(4) Love is set apart (vv. 8-11)

"Remember the sabbath day, to keep it holy. Six days shalt thou labor and do all thy work; but the seventh day is the sabbath of the Lord thy God; in it thou shalt not do any work, thou, nor thy son, nor thy daughter, thy manservant, nor thy maidservant, nor thy cattle, nor thy stranger that is within thy gates; for in six days the Lord made heaven and earth, the sea, and all that in them is, and rested the seventh day; wherefore, the Lord blessed the sabbath day, and halloweth it."

If I love somebody totally, I am set apart to that person only, right? If I say I love the Lord my God with all my heart, soul, mind, and strength, but I'm going to take the one day I'm supposed to spend worshiping Him and go do something else, that doesn't say much for my love, does it? Love separates itself totally to its object. When a man loves a woman, he will ultimately say, "I want you to be my wife. I love you so much I just want to separate myself to you. I'm not interested in any other woman, it's you that matters." That's love.

So, the Decalogue isn't some legalistic code of externals. It is merely a way to define love toward God and love:

b) Affecting our relationships with others

(1) Love is respectful (v. 12)

"Honor thy father and thy mother, that thy days may be long upon the land which the Lord thy God giveth thee."

In a sense, when you come into the world, your first neighbors are your parents. And the Bible simply says you are to love them with respect and honor. Love is never lawless or disorderly, but always respectful.

(2) Love is humane (v. 13)

"Thou shalt not kill."

If you love somebody, are you going to kill him? No. If you love your neighbor you won't do that because, as Paul said, "love is the fulfilling of the law" (Rom. 13:10*b*).

(3) Love is pure (v. 14)

"Thou shalt not commit adultery."

If you really love your spouse, you're not going to do that, because love is pure. Love doesn't defile. When a guy says to a girl, "I love you," and then tries to shove her in bed even though she's not his wife, that isn't love—love seeks purity. Don't tell your wife you love her and then go off and sleep with somebody else. If you do that, you don't love your wife—you're lying. True love is pure. It doesn't defile; it only exalts and maintains one's purity.

(4) Love is unselfish (v. 15)

"Thou shalt not steal."

If you love somebody, are you going to take what he has? No, you're not going to steal from somebody if you love him.

(5) Love is truthful (v. 16)

"Thou shalt not bear false witness against thy neighbor."

Are you going to tell lies or gossip about people if you love them? Of course not.

(6) Love is contented (v. 17)

"Thou shalt not covet thy neighbor's house; thou shalt not covet thy neighbor's wife, nor his manservant, nor his maidservant, nor his ox, nor his ass, nor anything that is thy neighbor's."

When you really love people, you don't covet what belongs to them, because you are glad they have it.

Now do you see the point of the Ten Commandments? They are merely a regulation of love—that's all. Once God established a relationship with His people, the law was provided as a way to define how that love worked, both toward God and toward one's neighbor. This outworking of the law in love was the epitome of the Old Testament in the book of Deuteronomy, which is no different than what Jesus and the epistles in the New Testament teach: The whole law is to love God and love your neighbor. Love toward God is loyal, faithful, reverent, and set apart; and love expressed toward one's neighbor is respectful of authority, respectful of life made in His image, pure, unselfish, truthful, and contented. And notice that every single one of those is rooted in a heart attitude, isn't it? Commandments like "Thou shalt not kill" and "Thou shalt not commit adultery" are much deeper and broader statements than the scribes and the Pharisees ever allowed for. They were simply statements of law regulating a heart attitude. And the sad thing that happened in Israel was that the Jews began to focus only on the external ritual and their religious observance, so that morality became a matter of what one did rather than a relationship of love. Thus they missed the whole point of the law.

Now, if you understand this, then you also understand the background of the Sermon on the Mount as it relates to:

III. THE SATISFACTION OF GOD'S LAW

In Matthew 5:21, when Jesus says, "Ye have heard that it was said by them of old, Thou shalt not kill and whosoever shall kill shall be in danger of judgment," He reveals the Jews' superficial approach to the law. They merely said that if one didn't kill, he was all right. But Jesus carried the intent of the law beyond the action to the attitude: "If you're angry with your brother, you are in danger of hell, because you don't love your brother, and that's the major issue with God. Similarly, you have heard them say that you shouldn't commit adultery; but I'm telling you that if you lust in your heart, you are guilty, because your attitude toward your brother is wrong. You are not pure, and you're coveting something that isn't yours." Now this is the whole background of what Jesus was saying. He drives the Jews down deep to the matter of the heart, forcing them to recognize:

A. The Prominence of Sin

The tradition of the Jews had obscured the original message of God and corrupted it. Their reaction to the law that Jesus was reiterating was just the same as the Jews of old would say: "We can't keep that law. It can't be done—we're not that good. We can't love like that all the time. We need help, we can't maintain that standard of God's." And that is exactly what He wants them to say. In the Old Testament, when they couldn't maintain it, they participated in the sacrificial system.

B. The Provision of a Sacrifice

Ultimately, the sacrificial system consummated in Jesus Christ, who was slain as the Lamb of God to take away the sin of the world (John 1:29). Of Him, the writer of Hebrews says, "For by one offering he hath perfected forever them that are sanctified" (Heb. 10:14). Jesus did what the blood of bulls and goats could never do—take away sin. That is why after He died on the cross and paid the final penalty, judgment was brought upon the city of Jerusalem in A.D. 70. The Romans came into the city of Jerusalem and literally destroyed the Temple, thus fully destroying the sacrificial system, which had been symbolically ended with the ripping of the veil when Jesus died (Matt. 27:51). Since that time, there has never been a sacrificial system in Israel, because that to which it pointed had arrived—Jesus Christ. The ultimate sacrifice of Jesus Christ took away the sin that all the systems of sacrifices could never take away, but simply pointed to.

C. The Plan of Salvation

You say, "Well, then, how would that person in the Old Testament be saved?" The efficacy of Christ's death went forward to us and backward to them. If they believed God when they lived, looking forward to the fact that God would take away their sin by His power, and realizing they couldn't become righteous on their own, then they would be saved through the sacrifice of Christ, even though He had not been offered yet. As for us, we are on this end of the sacrifice of Christ, and though He died two thousand years ago, His sacrifice is applied to us today if we believe and accept Him. In frustration, we must recognize our inability to keep the exalted law of God and run for mercy to Jesus Christ, who alone can grant us a righteousness we cannot obtain on our own. In 2 Corinthians 5:21, Paul sums it up in these words: "For he [God] hath made him [Christ], who knew no sin, to be sin for us, that we might be made the righteousness of God in him." In other words, we couldn't be righteous, because we were sinful. It was necessary for Him to bear our sins that we might be declared righteous.

Conclusion

The words of this covenant that cemented the relationship in the Old Testament were not legalistic, they simply established a standard by which a loving relationship to God and your neighbor could be directed. There had to be the relationship first, or all the law keeping that went on meant absolutely nothing. This is true today, too. There are people in our society who live by New Testament ethics, who are good fathers and mothers and neighbors, who give to charity, go to church, don't kill people, don't commit adultery, and who keep the outward law, but who don't have a love relationship with God. In their cases, the law means nothing, because it isn't the outworking of love. It is the inner attitude that has always been the issue with God, whether it's the Old or the New Testament that is in view. That's why Jesus could say, "I didn't come to destroy the prophets or to set Moses aside. I didn't come to change one single thing—only to put the law back where it belongs. And unless you get up to that level, which is higher than the scribes and Pharisees, you will never under any circumstances enter My kingdom." Of course, we realize we can't fully attain God's standard, and that forces us to Christ. In like manner, Moses was pointing the Israelites to Jesus just as Jesus was pointing them to Himself. In fact in Luke 16:15, Jesus says to the Pharisees who were so covetous in their hearts, "Ye are they who justify yourselves before men, but God knoweth your hearts; for that which is highly esteemed among men is abomination in the sight of God." It is an abomination to God to keep an external law without a heart relationship. God knows your hearts.

So our Lord simply redefines the original standard, and in so doing He defines righteousness and sin in true biblical terms. This is so important. If you don't understand sin, you'll never understand anything else in the Scripture. It was a subject that Jesus spent a tremendous amount of time dealing with. And it was a reality that John Newton never forgot. When he was an old man and his memory was nearly gone, this great saint still remembered: first, that he was a great sinner, and second, that Jesus Christ is a great Savior. That's the issue. That's what Jesus wanted the Pharisees to see, and that is what He wants you to see—you were so great a sinner in God's eyes that you couldn't atone for your sin. Therefore, He did it for you.

I read once about a child who was bitten by a poisonous snake. Because the mother was there when the child was bitten, she desperately placed her lips over the wound to suck the poison out. However, though she succeeded in saving the child's life, she lost her own because the poison entered into her through a cut on her lip. So it was with Jesus Christ, who drained out of us, as it were, the poison of the serpent, and in so doing, died in our place. We are great sinners, but He is a great Savior.

Focusing on the Facts

1. Who were supposedly the most righteous people in the Jewish society? What kind of righteousness did Jesus require in relation to them (see p. 41)?
2. Though the scribes and Pharisees claimed to be the proponents of the law of Moses, what had they actually done to that law (see p. 41)?
3. Explain why man tries to create God in his own image (see p. 41).
4. What was Jesus trying to destroy by reestablishing God's original standard (see p. 42)?
5. God was never solely concerned about the _____, but rather primarily the _____ behind it (see p. 42).
6. What similarities can we see between Greek and Roman paganism and our society today (see p. 43)?
7. Identify and describe the new morality that has been espoused by some church men and philosophers (see pp. 44-45).
8. Describe the Corinthians' wrong perspective on sex that Paul confronted (see p. 45).
9. Why are viewing sex as shameful and as purely a biological function both equally perverted perspectives (see p. 46)?
10. What realization should have driven Jesus' audience into desperation to seek God (see p. 47)?
11. Essentially, what is the core of the Old Testament? Why (see pp. 48-49)?
12. What Old Testament book contains a summary of the law of God and even the entire Bible (see pp. 48-49)?
13. Identify the principle that is the pinnacle of the whole Bible (see p. 49).
14. Rather than building a relationship on law, on what does the Old Testament build (see p. 49)?
15. Before God ever gave the law to Israel, what did He establish (see p. 50)?
16. What should characterize the response of one brought into a relationship of love with God (see p. 50)?
17. What were the two alternatives that Moses offered Israel (see p. 51)?
18. What were the Ten Commandments given to regulate (see p. 53)?
19. What does God want people to recognize about His standard (see pp. 53-54).
20. What did God provide for those in the Old Testament as a way of dealing with their inability to keep His standard (see p. 54)?
21. To whom did the sacrificial system point? Why. (see p. 54)?
22. Which of the Ten Commandments relate to our love for God and

which relate to our love for our neighbor (see p. 55)?

23. Express each of the Ten Commandments in positive terms of love (see pp. 55-57).
24. When the Jews began to focus only on the external ritual and their religious observance, what did morality become (see p. 58)?
25. In the Old Testament, when the people couldn't maintain God's standard, what did they do (see p. 59)?
26. What two events following the death of Christ showed that His death had replaced the sacrificial system for taking away sin (see p. 59)?
27. How were people in the Old Testament saved (see p. 59)?

Pondering the Principles

1. Meditate upon Matthew 5:29-30. In one short sentence, explain what Jesus is trying to teach in this hyperbole. Though sin has serious consequences and we are exhorted to deal with it in drastic measures, do you find yourself toying with it to see how far you can get without being caught? Does your own response to sin in your life reflect what Jesus says about it? If not, what changes do you need to make so that you can say with Paul, "How shall we, that are dead to sin, live any longer in it?" (Rom. 6:2).
2. Do you agree that sexual temptation is getting worse in our society? With the constant visual bombardment of sexual temptation through the media, what steps could you take to avoid unnecessary enticement? For some suggestions, read the following: Genesis 39:7-12; Philippians 4:4-8; and 1 Corinthians 6:18—7:5.
3. Is your relationship with God legalistic or loving? Do you see God more as a Judge or as a Father? In the parable of the Prodigal Son, which son do you think loved his Father more from the standpoint of legal obedience? Which one loved out of gratefulness? If someone asked you why you loved God, what would you say? If you have never done so, memorize Matthew 22:37-40 and recite it each day for a week before you go to sleep and as you wake up.
4. Those who believe in life after death generally look forward to some form of heaven. However, like the Pharisees, their requirements for entrance are far lower than God's. Rehearse in your own mind what you would say to someone who told you they were going to go to heaven because they had been pretty good. For some verses to stimulate your thinking, read the following: Psalm 143:2; Proverbs 20:9; Ecclesiastes 7:20; Romans 3:9-28; 5:12-13; Galatians 2:16; and Ephesians 2:1-10. Who are some people in your sphere of influence who are religious, yet don't really seem to know God? Pray that God would give you some opportunities to share with them some of the truths and principles that you have learned or that have been reinforced in this study.

4

Who Is an Adulterer?—Part 2

Outline

Introduction
A. The Relationship of Sin to Salvation
B. The Relationship of Sin to Sharing
   1. Superficial approaches to evangelism
   2. Scriptural application of evangelism
     a) The summary
     b) The specifics
       (1) The pattern of Paul
       (2) The preaching of Jesus
C. The Relationship of Sin to Sanctification
   1. The superficial perspective
   2. The scriptural perspective
     a) Proverbs 23:7
     b) Matthew 15:16-19
     c) Jeremiah 17:9

Lesson
 I. The Deed
   A. Its Condemnation
     1. In scriptural teaching
     2. In scribal tradition
   B. Its Clarification
   C. Its Consequences
II. The Desire
   A. The Passage Examined
     1. "But I"
     2. "Whosoever looketh"
     3. "Hath . . . already"
     4. "To lust"
   B. The Process Explained
     1. Succumbing to temptation
     2. Sowing the temptation
     3. Shunning the temptation

III. The Deliverance
   A. Removing the Offense to Sin
     1. The passage explained
     2. The parallel examined
     3. The problem eliminated
     4. The picture expressed
   B. Recognizing the Offering of the Savior

Introduction

As Jesus gave a message on the divine definition of sin, the truth of Numbers 32:23, "Be sure your sin will find you out," was experienced by the Jewish leaders and the rest of the people listening to Him. Jesus unmasked their hypocrisy, revealing the truth about the sinful heart of man. They had done what man has always done—invented a self-righteous system of human achievement that is based on their own standards, thereby enabling them to justify themselves. The Judaism of Jesus' day had substituted their own external rules for the divine standard that took into account the motive of the heart. For that reason, Jesus faced them with a standard they couldn't keep because of the problem of sin for which they had no remedy. He said, "Be ye, therefore, perfect, even as your Father, who is in heaven, is perfect" (Matt. 5:48), demanding a righteousness for His kingdom that they could never attain on their own. In that way, He was forcing them to see their need of a Savior, knowing full well He would offer Himself as that Savior. He began to accomplish that by contrasting their definition of sin with God's definition of sin, and their standard of righteousness with the divine standard. Revealing that God has always been primarily concerned about the heart and a relationship of love, Jesus showed that the commandment of God was a lot broader than they thought—they had narrowed it down only to the external, and our Lord brought it in to the internal.

In His Sermon on the Mount, Jesus began with a message about blessedness in 5:3-12. However, in order for His listeners to know that blessedness, He realized that they also needed to understand the proper definition of sin, because sin stands in the way of blessing, and therefore has to be dealt with and removed. And so from blessedness to a doctrine of sin the Lord makes a transition.

Now let me just say in general before we look at the passage itself that it's essential to deal with sin. You cannot preach Christ and present the gospel unless you deal with sin and give its proper definition, because sin is the barrier between God and man. If we do not properly understand sin, we will not understand anything else that God does. It is important to see:

A. The Relationship of Sin to Salvation

Unless one understands the truth about sin, he can never understand the truth about salvation. The Pharisees and the scribes had such a superficial view of sin that they were able to accommodate it with a superficial view of salvation. They saw sin as simply a matter of what one did; therefore salvation also became a matter of what one did. So in their minimal definition of sin, they were left with a minimal requirement for salvation, which they then assumed they could accomplish. Had they seen sin as a problem deep down in the heart, they would have known that it was far beyond their ability to change.

The more we comprehend the heinousness of sin, the more we understand the necessity of salvation—the deeper the disease, the greater the remedy. As long as people think of sin superficially, then salvation is a minor thing too. But when you understand, as our Lord is saying, that sin is something heinous that penetrates into the warp and woof of a man's being so deeply that it is absolutely unchangeable except by a miracle, then you'll understand that only God can bring salvation. Sin is so powerful and so deeply entrenched in man, that only Jesus Christ can change it. That is the message of Romans 3-6.

B. The Relationship of Sin to Sharing

Second, unless you understand the truth about sin, you will never understand the right approach to the proclamation of the gospel.

1. Superficial approaches to evangelism

What we have in our Christian culture today are very superficial gospel presentations with emphases upon methodology and obtaining pie-in-the-sky happiness. Some call it "easy believism," others call it "cheap grace." There are people running around with self-centered, emotional appeals. I really feel that behind this is a failure to grapple with the reality of the heinousness of sin, because if we understand the power of sin, then we know it isn't enough to tell somebody, "Why don't you just accept Jesus and He'll make your life happy? Would you like to go to heaven and be happy and have peace and joy and everything? Just sign on the dotted line and say you believe in Jesus and pray a little prayer."

2. Scriptural application of evangelism

a) The summary

If we really understood how deeply stained with sin men's hearts are and how powerful the hold of sin is so that it casts men into an eternal hell, then our evangelism would be more directed at the damning character of sin before it comes to the point of inviting them to make a decision. Those with whom we share Christ must understand the problem, which is why, biblically speaking, evangelism always begins by presenting the law before grace. You must present the reality of judgment and condemnation for sin so that people understand the need for salvation.

b) The specifics

(1) The pattern of Paul

We should follow the pattern of Romans, which begins this way: "For the wrath of God is revealed from heaven against all ungodliness and unrighteousness of men" (Rom. 1:18*a*). Paul starts out by condemning in chapter 1 and condemns again in chapters 2 and 3 so that "every mouth may be stopped, and all the world may become guilty before God" (Rom. 3:19*b*). Then comes the good news about the righteousness of Christ that is available to us. There must be a preaching of the divine standard of the holy law before there can be the message of how we come to know the relationship with Christ that makes that possible. Consequently, I believe our evangelism must confront people with the holiness of God. It must reveal His demands for a heart righteousness, focusing on man's inability to meet God's standard. We must make men desperate—as Jesus wanted to make the Pharisees, the scribes, and the multitude—so that they stand in fear of the doom of judgment, crying out for a Savior who can deliver them from a problem too deep for them to handle.

(2) The preaching of Jesus

That was Jesus' approach. It was basically designed to drive men to desperation. More than anybody else in the whole Bible, Jesus preached about hell. People don't like to even talk about it, but He preached that sin sends people to an eternal hell, "where their worm dieth not, and the fire is not quenched" (Mark 9:44), and where "there shall be wailing and gnashing of teeth" (Matt. 13:42*b*). Jesus preached about hell, because that's where the understanding of the gospel had to begin.

Evangelism and proclamation must start with the holiness of God and the sinfulness of man. Only then will the demands of that holy God show hopeless and helpless man, who can't fulfill them, the inevitability of punishment and the ultimate reality of hell. Then, when a sinner understands that the only escape is for someone else to come along and change his vile heart, Jesus Christ can move in and offer the deliverance that He alone is able to give.

C. The Relationship of Sin to Sanctification

1. The superficial perspective

Unless we understand the meaning of sin, we don't know what it is to be made holy in Christ. We don't fully appreciate the tremendous change God has accomplished in us through Christ unless we know what we once were. We can't be thanking and praising Him for that glorious transformation unless we know what an incredible price God paid. Usually, we think we're holy because of the things we do or don't do. So we don't go to certain places, we don't say certain things, and we don't do the things the world does, believing, therefore, that we are all right. But that is nothing more than the ugly head of self-righteousness, because God is concerned not so much with what we do and say and where we go as He is with what is behind our words and actions—what we think in our minds and hearts. There are the pious and self-satisfied who smugly think that because they don't do certain things and do do other things that they are justified, without ever really examining the evil of their hearts.

2. The scriptural perspective

As He preaches this great sermon, the Lord Jesus is forcing men to examine their hearts, because holiness is always a matter of the heart.

a) Proverbs 23:7—"For as he thinketh in his heart, so is he." That's where the divine evaluation takes place.

b) Matthew 15:16-19—"And Jesus said, Are ye also yet without understanding? Do not ye yet understand, that whatsoever entereth in at the mouth goeth into the stomach, and is cast out into the draught [the process of elimination]? But those things which proceed out of the mouth come forth from the heart, and they defile the man. For out of the heart proceed evil thoughts, murders, adulteries, fornications, thefts, false witness, blasphemies."

Where do those all originate? In the heart. Before you ever murder, commit adultery, fornicate, or steal, you think it in your heart. It is the heart that spews out the garbage that defiles man because of its natural wickedness, as indicated in:

 c) Jeremiah 17:9—"The heart is deceitful above all things, and desperately wicked; who can know it?"

So our Lord bares the heart, ripping off the facade of the super-religious who would glorify themselves as if they stood absolved and showing them that the primary thing He is concerned with is the heart. His message is the same as that found in the Old Testament—man is a sinner, and that sin is deep down in his heart. Powerless to change that, man is dependent upon God to change his heart, who said through the prophet Ezekiel, "And I will give them one heart, and I will put a new spirit within you; and I will take the stony heart out of their flesh, and will give them an heart of flesh" (11:19). A new heart is what a man needs, and that's what Jesus wants those who are listening to understand. Let's examine how He illustrates this truth with the issue of adultery.

Lesson

I. THE DEED (v. 27)

"Ye have heard that it was said by them of old, Thou shalt not commit adultery."

A. Its Condemnation

1. In scriptural teaching

   Exodus 20:14 states this prohibition, and Deuteronomy 5:18 repeats it: "Neither shalt thou commit adultery." It's very clear—the Bible leaves absolutely no question about this particular sin. The deed is condemned as a wicked manifestation of an evil heart for which the penalty of death was given (Lev. 20:10). So, the Bible clearly teaches that the deed is condemned by God.

2. In scribal tradition

   You will notice that in our passage in Matthew, it was the rabbinic tradition that had taught "thou shalt not commit adultery." Even they were right. I am not implying that they were wrong, I am only saying that they never went far enough. They admitted that it was a serious crime that God forbade.

B. Its Clarification

Let me define the word *adultery* for a better understanding. The root means "unlawful intercourse with the spouse of someone else." Many Bible scholars understand this to be not only a command not to engage in sexual activity with somebody else's spouse but also a general command against any type of illicit sexual activity, because the word is also used in a general way in some other places. For example, in some ancient sources, the word means "to seduce or violate a woman, whether married or unmarried." Other places it is translated "to commit harlotry." In a general sense, the word has been used to speak of any kind of illicit intercourse at all outside the bond of marriage. Though primarily it refers to a sexual relationship that violates a marriage, I believe the spirit of it extends further to include any kind of illicit sexual behavior.

I think the broader definition is indicated in verse 28 when our Lord says that anybody who looks on any woman "to lust after her hath committed adultery with her already in his heart." And the woman He speaks of here isn't identified as being married or not. The context is broad enough to imply that anybody who lusts after any woman has committed adultery in his heart.

C. Its Consequences

Adultery is a sin that really waves the banner today. It's as if we've just completely turned our backs on the seriousness of the sin. People ought to read Proverbs 5-7 before they ever engage in it, because that passage speaks so pointedly to the devastation caused by the sin of adultery or fornication. It is a sin of fools. Witness David and the results in his life; or Shechem, who defiled Dinah and was later slaughtered; or Absalom, who defiled others with sexual sin and wound up being hanged in a tree. The Bible says that when you commit this sin you take fire into your bosom (Prov. 6:27).

Furthermore, it says that "fornicators and adulterers God will judge" (Heb. 13:4b). The New Testament reiterates with finality and firmness this condemnation of adultery in such passages as 1 Corinthians 6:9-10, 2 Peter 2:14, and Revelation 2:21-23; and Revelation 22:15 says that fornicators and adulterers won't even enter into God's kingdom. And sexual immorality today is just as vile, heinous, and evil as it was then. I don't care if you're engaged and you believe you love each other—whenever sexual union occurs apart from the bond of monogamous heterosexual marriage, it is a heinous crime against God and man. This really needs to be said in our day because people don't believe it.

So the deed is first identified by Jesus, and then He turns to:

II. THE DESIRE (v. 28)

"But I say unto you that whosoever looketh on a woman to lust after her hath committed adultery with her already in his heart."

Now this is a fascinating verse, and there's much I want you to see in it. The Lord forces the self-righteous to realize the fact that they're not really holy. The Pharisees were saying, "We don't commit that sin." But Jesus drives right down into their hearts to reveal the truth of Psalm 66:18: "If I regard iniquity in my heart, the Lord will not hear me." God is always examining the sin of the heart, which breaks the relationship between Him and man. And so it is that Jesus is concerned about what's on the inside.

A. The Passage Examined

Let's look at some of the terms in this verse.

1. "But I"

This is emphatic in the Greek with the use of pronoun *egō*. Jesus is saying in contrast, "I am the new authority; you have had your authority in the rabbinic tradition. Sometimes it was true to Moses, though sometimes it was not." In fact, He was speaking in such a manner that when He was finished with the sermon, they were shocked because He spoke with such authority (Matt. 7:28-29).

2. "Whosoever looketh"

The present participle *blepōn* conveys the idea of a continuing process of looking. It isn't the inadvertent, accidental glance—that's not what our Lord is talking about. The purposeful, repeated, lustful looking is what is in view here.

3. "Hath . . . already"

There is an interesting thing I want you to notice about this verse. Jesus doesn't say that the one who lusts after a woman commits adultery at that point. Rather, He says that whoever looks on a woman to lust after her *has already* committed adultery in his heart, because it is the vile, adulterous heart that results in the wanton look. The sin has already happened in the heart—the adultery is conceived and thus the look is prompted.

You may find that someone passes into your gaze involuntarily as a possible temptation from Satan trying to entice you to sin. But whereas an involuntary glance means you just resist it and turn away, a lustful stare takes place when you culti-vate and pursue the sinful desire. Lust is the manifestation of an adulterous heart that is seeking an object to fulfill its fantasy.

4. "To lust"

In the Greek, "to lust" appears as *pros to* with the infinitive, which indicates purpose. In other words, this isn't an invol-untary glance; it is a purposeful one. The heart is filled with adultery wanting to find an object to attach the fantasy to. For example, you are looking for a woman to lust after if you go see an X-rated movie or you go around the dial on the television to find the thing that panders your lust, because you would be viewing with the purpose of filling the adulter-ous desire in your heart.

The verse, then, could be paraphrased this way: "Emphati-cally I say to you that whoever continues looking on a wom-an for the purpose of lusting gives evidence of already com-mitting adultery in his heart." The continued look is the manifestation of the vile heart.

So, Jesus is saying that the heart is the problem, because when a man purposefully looks on a woman to lust after her, he gives evidence of having a vile, lusting, and adulterous attitude. Therefore, it is the heart that has to be transformed from one that would look upon a woman as an object to gratify its adul-terous bent.

B. The Process Explained

1. Succumbing to temptation

Temptation to illicit sexual desire or fantasy is not sin in itself. Satan may tempt you, but the sin only comes in rela-tion to what you do with the temptation. If you entertain the temptation, pandering those evil thoughts, then it becomes sin. A biblical example of temptation giving birth to sin is found in 2 Samuel 11, where David is walking on his roof. Looking over the side, he sees Bathsheba bathing. She may have never dreamed that she could be seen from the king's palace toward evening. But instead of turning away and go-ing back inside, David continues to look until his adulterous heart brings forth an adulterous lust, ultimately ending in the act of adultery and the murder of Bathsheba's husband.

2. Sowing the temptation

This process of a temptation becoming a sin is well illustrated in the saying, "Sow a thought and reap an act, sow an act and

71

reap a habit, sow a habit and reap a character, sow a character and reap a destiny." It all starts when you sow a thought. The Bible says, "Unto the pure all things are pure, but unto them that are defiled and unbelieving is nothing pure" (Titus 1:15). A person can take something beautiful and make it something ugly because his heart is defiled. We can see this in the abuse of divinely designed sexual relations. For instance, pornography has in this way permeated every facet of the media and communication—books, magazines, movies, music, television shows, jokes, stories, and so on. Those things become proponents of the abuse of sex, because the heart of man is so evil that it finds ways to pander its adulterous desires.

A. W. Pink has said, "If lustful looking be so grievous a sin, then those who dress and expose themselves with desires to be looked at and lusted after—as Jezebel, who painted her face, tired her head, and looked out of the window (II Kings ix, 30)—are not less, but even more guilty. In this matter it is only too often the case that men sin, but women tempt them so to do. How great, then, must be the guilt of the great majority of the modern misses who deliberately seek to arouse the sexual passions of our young men. And how much greater still is the guilt of most of their mothers for allowing them to become lascivious temptresses" (*An Exposition of the Sermon on the Mount* [Grand Rapids: Baker, 1953], p. 83). Though our Lord is talking about a man lusting after a woman in His illustration, the assumption is accurate that women also can be as guilty as men by creating the temptation in the way that they dress.

3. Shunning the temptation

I actually fear sometimes when summer comes, because of the impropriety of some people in the way they dress. I don't think it assists the worship of the Lord, and therefore, I am always concerned about that, hoping that other believers are prayerful about their appearance as well. It is no wonder Job said, "I made a covenant with mine eyes. When then should I think upon a maid? . . . If my step hath turned out of the way, and mine heart walked after mine eyes, and if any blot hath cleaved to mine hands, then let me sow, and let another eat" (31:1, 7-8*a*). In other words, "If I break the covenant with my eyes not to look lustfully upon a woman, then let me starve." Job recognized that the thought is father to the deed, and that if he allowed his eyes the privilege, they would pander his adulterous heart. His prayer is like that in Psalm 119:37: "Turn away mine eyes from beholding vanity."

So our Lord is saying that the heart has to be dealt with, because the heart is the root of sin. But He doesn't leave us in a hopeless situation; He goes a step further to answer the question, "How do you get out of this situation?"

III. THE DELIVERANCE (vv. 29-30)

"And if thy right eye offend thee, pluck it out, and cast it from thee; for it is profitable for thee that one of thy members should perish, and not that thy whole body should be cast into hell. And if thy right hand offend thee, cut it off, and cast it from thee; for it is profitable for thee that one of thy members should perish, and not that thy whole body should be cast into hell."

A. Removing the Offense to Sin

1. The passage explained

Now when you first read that you say, "Well, that's absolutely incongruous. If He has just said that the issue is the heart, why is He now saying, 'Pluck out the eye'? Wouldn't a person who had lost his eyesight still be able to lust?" You'd better believe it! If you plucked out your right eye and got rid of your right hand, your heart would still be able to lust. Jesus is not saying that there is a physical remedy for a heart problem—that would undermine the whole point. Because the right eye, arm, and leg were symbols of the best facilities that a man had, Jesus is simply saying that there is nothing too precious to eliminate from your life if it is going to cause your heart to be pandered in its adulterous desires. If it means getting rid of your most precious possession, then get rid of it, even if it's your right eye or your right arm.

2. The parallel examined

A similar passage appears in Matthew 18:7-9: "Woe unto the world because of offenses! For it must needs be that offenses come; but woe to that man by whom the offense cometh! Wherefore, if thy hand or thy foot offend thee, cut it off, and cast it from thee; it is better for thee to enter into life lame or maimed, rather than, having two hands or two feet, to be cast into everlasting fire. And if thine eye offend thee, pluck it out, and cast it from thee; it is better for thee to enter into life with one eye, rather than, having two eyes, to be cast into hell fire." Jesus is teaching that anything that causes a man to remain in his sin and to pander an adulterous and evil heart should be eliminated, even if it is something you wouldn't dream of giving up.

73

3. The problem eliminated

People come along and say, "I'm leaving my wife, because I've found another woman. We're in love—oh, she means everything to me!" I say, "Dump her! Get rid of her! You're pandering your lust and condemning your soul." Our Lord is saying that nothing is precious if it affects your eternal destiny. Sin must be dealt with radically. This is why Paul says, "I keep under [beat] my body, and bring it into subjection" (1 Cor. 9:27a). Similarly, Jesus calls for immediate action and effective action against sin. He diagnoses the problem and says, "Pluck it out, cut it off, eliminate it—whatever it is in your life that feeds that heart of lust—get rid of it!" If you go to a theater and you watch something that nurtures adulterous thoughts, then get out. If you have that problem with your television, get rid of it. If you read things that incite sinful thoughts, throw them in the trash. Jesus is not really talking about the physical—we know that. He knows that cutting off your right hand or plucking out your right eye isn't going to change an adulterous heart. But what He is saying is that you should take the most precious thing you have—your right arm, your right eye, if need be—and get rid of it if it stands in the way of purity and brings you to sin.

4. The picture expressed

Notice the word "offend" (Gk., *skandalon*) in verses 29 and 30. In the Greek, the word is used literally of a bait stick in a trap, where an animal would come and grab the bait on the bait stick and the trap would close. In this context, it is as though Jesus is saying, "If your right eye is the bait stick that catches you in the trap where your adulterous lust is fulfilled, then pluck it out. If your right hand causes you to be trapped, then cut it off. Whatever it is in your life that causes these vile, evil thoughts, get rid of it."

B. Recognizing the Offering of the Savior

Now there's a subtlety in the solution Jesus gives, because the immediate solution points up the need for a permanent solution. Could these scribes and Pharisees get rid of their sinful hearts? The fact of the matter is, they couldn't. Jesus again is giving them an impossible standard, a frustration that is going to make them say, "We tried and we couldn't. We hear you say it's better to have one eye and one arm and have life, than to go into hell. But we don't know how to get this deliverance. We are desperate—we must have somebody show us how to obtain a new heart and a new life." And that is precisely what the Lord offers:

> A heart in every thought renewed
> and filled with love divine,
> Perfect and right and pure and good,
> A copy, Lord, of Thine.

The Lord forces them to see that they need a new nature.

If Jesus Christ has come into your life, you have that new nature—you have that new heart. You don't need to fall prey to the sins of lust and adultery—you can know victory over them. I thank God for that. Like Job, you can make a covenant with your eyes, and as Colossians 3:5 says, you can kill the members of your body in this world. You can know victory over those sins that constantly victimize men and women who do not know Jesus Christ. Oh, how grateful we should be that what the Lord has given us is a resource for victory. I thank God that He's given us who know Him new hearts so that we are not left defenseless in the constant battle against sin. We never need to lose if we appropriate the resources that are there.

Focusing on the Facts

1. What had the Jews of Jesus' day substituted for the divine standard (see p. 64)?
2. In demanding a righteousness the people could never attain, what was Jesus forcing them to realize (see p. 64)?
3. What is it that stands in the way of blessing and must be dealt with and removed (see p. 64)?
4. What are three things we will never fully understand unless we first understand sin (see pp. 65-67)?
5. The Jews' minimal definition of sin resulted in a minimal requirement for _____ (see p. 65).
6. In sharing the gospel with others, why must we present the reality of judgment and condemnation for sin (see p. 66)?
7. What did Jesus preach about that was designed to drive men to desperation (see p. 66)?
8. Where do unrighteous actions originate, according to Matthew 15:16-19 (see pp. 67-68)?
9. Because man is powerless to change his sinful heart, whom is he dependent upon to change it (see p. 68)?
10. What was the penalty for committing adultery in the Old Testament (see p. 68)?
11. Compare the technical and the general definitions of adultery (see p. 69).

12. When is a sexual union a heinous crime against God (see p. 69)?
13. What results from sin in the heart, as indicated by Psalm 66:18 (see p. 70)?
14. Because verse 28 indicates a continuing process of looking, what type of look is not being condemned by Jesus (see p. 70)?
15. According to verse 28, when did the one in view commit adultery—before, during, or after the looking (see p. 71)?
16. What is one manifestation of an adulterous heart that is seeking an object to fulfill its fantasy (see p. 71)?
17. Is temptation sin? If not, when does it become sin (see p. 71)?
18. What was David's mistake in facing the temptation of Bathsheba (see p. 71)?
19. Though a woman may not lust in the same way a man does, how can she participate in its guilt (see p. 72)?
20. What did Job recognize about the process of lusting? What preventative measures did he take, according to Job 31:1 (see p. 72)?
21. In verses 29-30, is Jesus saying there is a physical remedy for a heart problem? Paraphrase these verses in your own words (see pp. 73-74).

Pondering the Principles

1. Has your approach to evangelism been superficial? Have you included a proper and necessary understanding of how sin separates all men from a holy God? Have you included the consequences of eternal death in hell for all sinners who reject the merciful salvation Christ offers? Which do you think would be a better result of your sharing of the gospel—someone who fully understands what he is rejecting or someone who thinks he is a Christian merely because you shared the gospel with him? Which one would have the best possibility of reaching out to Jesus at a future date? Which one would probably see no need for reevaluating his spiritual life again? Why? If it has been a while since you have actively shared the gift of Christ with someone, pray that God would open opportunities in your sphere of influence to do so. Take a few minutes to brainstorm on two or three phrases you might use to direct a conversation toward spiritual things and ultimately the gospel as the perfect solution to man's problems. (You might even want to enroll in an evangelism seminar or read some books on the subject to give you confidence in knowing what to say and how to say it.)
2. Take a moment and praise God that when you trusted in Him, He gave you a new heart, just as He promised He would give Israel one day (Ezek. 11:19).
3. Read Proverbs 2:1-22; 5:1-23; 6:20-35; and 7:1-27. Why do you think Solomon spent so much time on the issue of adultery? Describe some of the consequences that are given for committing adul-

tery. Identify some preventative measures for avoiding the sin. Knowing that there is absolutely no redeeming value in committing adultery but only devastating consequences, what are some of the verses from these passages that you could share with those you personally know who are involved in adulterous situations?

4. Are there things in your life that are nurturing adulterous thoughts? What immediate and drastic action should you take now as a preventative measure to avoid falling into sin when the temptation strikes full force? Meditate now upon Matthew 5:29-30 as you ask yourself if you are taking sin seriously enough. Make a point of doing this at least on a monthly basis.

5

Man's Biggest Problem

Outline

Introduction
A. The Confrontation of Sin
B. The Consequences of Sin
C. The Countenance of Sin
D. The Character of Sin

Lesson
 I. What Is Sin?
  A. Lawlessness
  B. Unrighteousness
  C. Failure to Do Good
  D. Lack of Faith
II. What Is Sin Like?
  A. Defilement
    1. Isaiah 30:22
    2. 1 Kings 8:38
    3. Zechariah 3:3
    4. Zechariah 11:8
    5. Ezekiel 20:43
    6. 2 Corinthians 7:1
  B. Rebellion
    1. Leviticus 26:27
    2. Hebrews 10:29
    3. Jeremiah 44:17
  C. Ingratitude
    1. Acts 17:28
    2. Matthew 5:45
    3. Samuel 16:15–17:4
  D. Incurable
    1. Jeremiah 13:23
    2. Isaiah 1:4-6
    3. Titus 1:15
  E. Hated by God
    1. Habakkuk 1:13

      2. Jeremiah 44:4
   F. Hard Work
      1. Jeremiah 9:5
      2. Psalm 7:14
      3. Proverbs 4:16
      4. Ezekiel 24:12
III. How Many People Does Sin Affect?
   A. Its Extent
      1. Romans 5:12
      2. Romans 3:23
      3. Romans 3:19
   B. Its Transmission
      1. Described
         a) Joshua 7
         b) Hebrews 7:9-10
         c) Job 14:4
         d) Psalm 58:3
         e) Psalm 51:5
      2. Debated
      3. Decided
         a) Romans 7:25
         b) Hebrews 12:1
IV. What Is the Result of Sin?
   A. Sin Causes Evil to Overpower Us
      1. Evil dominates the mind
         a) Jeremiah 17:9
         b) Ephesians 4:17-19
         c) 1 Corinthians 2:14
      2. Evil dominates the will
      3. Evil dominates the affections
         a) 1 John 2:15
         b) John 3:19
   B. Sin Brings Us Under the Control of Satan
      1. Ephesians 2:2
      2. John 8:44
      3. 1 John 5:19
      4. Romans 6:16
   C. Sin Makes Us the Objects of God's Wrath
      1. Ephesians 2:3
      2. Psalm 90:11
      3. Galatians 3:10-11
      4. 1 Corinthians 16:22
   D. Sin Subjects Us to the Miseries of Life
      1. Job 5:7
      2. Romans 8:20
      3. Ecclesiastes 1:2

Introduction

A. The Confrontation of Sin

It is said that a distinguished minister from Australia preached very strongly one day on the subject of sin. After the service, one of the church officers came to counsel with him in his study and he said, "Dr. Howard, we don't want you to talk as openly as you do about man's corruption, because if our boys and girls hear you discussing the subject, they will more easily become sinners. Call it a mistake if you will, but don't speak so plainly about sin." The minister took down a small bottle from the cabinet and showed it to the visitor and said, "Do you see that label? It says *strychnine,* and underneath that in bold red letters is the word *poison.* Do you know, man, what you are asking me to do? You're suggesting that I change the label. Suppose I do and paste over it the words *essence of peppermint.* Do you see what might happen? Someone would use it not knowing the danger involved and would die—and so it is too with the matter of sin. The milder you make the label, the more dangerous you make the poison." And so we cannot mitigate the danger of sin. We must speak of the issue.

B. The Consequences of Sin

Chrysostom, the early church Father, said he feared nothing but sin. I understand that, because that's exactly how I feel. I don't fear anything in the world or in the church except sin. Sin can destroy us, rob us of our power, confuse us, cast us upon the mercy of Satan, and ultimately damn the unregenerate to an eternal hell. The greatest problem facing man, the one great blight on human life that curses us all, is sin. It pervades the whole world, and only when it is removed will paradise be regained. That is why we find in Revelation 21:3-4 and in 2 Peter 3:13 that God has to do a work of purging the whole universe of

80

evil if ever there is to be paradise regained. Because of sin there are tears and pain. Because of sin there are wars and fighting, anxiety and discord, fear and worry, sickness and death, famines and earthquakes, and other manifestations of disharmony in nature.

Sin disturbs every relationship that exists in the human realm—that between man and God, man and nature, and man and man. You read Genesis 3 and you find that the curse came violating each of those relationships. First of all, man was separated from God when he became subject to spiritual death. Second, man was separated in a sense from nature, insofar as he had to toil by the sweat of his brow and fight against a cursed earth. Third, man was separated from man as the curse upon Adam and Eve brought conflict into their own marriage and between their sons. Sin waits lurking to attack every baby born into the world. David said, "In sin did my mother conceive me" (Ps. 51:5b). Sin rules every heart as the monarch of man and the lord of the soul from whom nobody ever escapes. All who die—whether from heart disease, cancer, war, murder, accidents, or any other cause—die as victims of sin, regardless of age, for Romans 6:23 says, "For the wages of sin is death." Every person on the globe has been infected with the virus of sin. Only one person ever entered this world and passed through it without the stain of sin—and that was Jesus Christ. Every other human being is captured under the fearful power of sin.

C. The Countenance of Sin

Sin is a destructive thing. This is vividly illustrated in a story told many years ago about Leonardo da Vinci. When Leonardo da Vinci was painting his great masterpiece known as *The Last Supper,* he sought long for a model for Jesus Christ. At last he located a chorister in one of the churches of Rome who was lovely in life and features, a young man named Pietro Bandinelli. Years passed, and the painting was still unfinished. All the disciples had been portrayed except one—Judas Iscariot. After all of those years, da Vinci began the search for a face that had been hardened and distorted by sin—and at last he found a beggar on the streets of Rome with a face so villainous he shuddered when he looked at him. He hired the man to sit for him as he painted the face of Judas on his canvas. When he was about to dismiss the man, he said, "I have not yet found out your name." "I am Pietro Bandinelli," he replied. "I also sat for you as your model for Christ." The sinful years had disfigured the face, and that's the way of sin.

D. The Character of Sin

Sin attacks everyone at birth and before it's done it degrades, debases, and destroys in an eternal hell. Every broken marriage, every disrupted home, every shattered friendship, every argument, every disagreement, every pain, and every tear can be attributed to sin. Referred to in Joshua 7:13 as "the accursed thing," sin is compared to the venom of snakes and the stench of death. Anything that is sinister and powerful must be faced and dealt with—and sin is such. We cannot ignore it, gloss it over, or change the label—we must face the reality of sin, and that is exactly what Jesus is saying.

"Who is the hoary sexton that digs man a grave? Who is the painted temptress that steals his virtue? Who is the murderess that destroys his life? Who is this sorceress that first deceives, and then damns his soul?—Sin. Who with icy breath, blights the fair blossoms of youth? Who breaks the hearts of parents? Who brings old men's gray hairs with sorrow to the grave?—Sin. Who, by a more hideous metamorphosis than Ovid even fancied, changes gentle children into vipers, tender mothers into monsters, and their fathers into worse than Herods, the murderers of their own innocents?—Sin. Who casts the apple of discord on household hearts? Who lights the torch of war, and bears it blazing over trembling lands? Who by divisions in the church, rends Christ's seamless robe?—Sin. Who is this Delilah that sings the Nazirite asleep, and delivers up the strength of God into the hands of the uncircumcised? Who, winning smiles on her face, honeyed flattery on her tongue, stands in the door to offer the sacred rites of hospitality, and when suspicion sleeps, treacherously pierces our temples with a nail? What fair Siren is this, who, seated on a rock by the deadly pool, smiles to deceive, sings to lure, kisses to betray, and flings her arm around our neck, to leap with us into perdition?—Sin. Who turns the soft and gentlest heart to stone? Who hurls reason from her lofty throne, and impels sinners, mad as Gadarene swine, down the precipice, into a lake of fire?—Sin."

Since all of this is true, we must understand sin. To help us do this, I would like to answer five questions.

Lesson

I. WHAT IS SIN?

Anything as severe as sin needs a definition so that we can understand it and thereby avoid it.

A. Lawlessness

The definition is simple. First John 3:4 says that "sin is the transgression of the law." Literally, the Greek says that everyone doing sin is doing lawlessness *(anomia).* Sin is disobeying or ignoring God's law. In fact, the grammatical construction of this verse makes sin and lawlessness identical. We might say that sin is living as if there were no God and no law. It is not being bound by the standards of God, it is living on your own terms.

Now, the Bible gives other definitions of sin as well, which include:

B. Unrighteousness

First John 5:17 says, "All unrighteousness is sin."

C. Failure to Do Good

James 4:17 says, "To him that knoweth to do good, and doeth it not, to him it is sin."

D. Lack of Faith

In Romans 14:23, we have yet another definition of sin: The apostle Paul says, "For whatever is not of faith is sin."

A lack of faith, an unrighteous act, not doing what you know you ought to do, can all be identified as sin, but it all can be summed up in this—sin is lawlessness. It is not responding to the law of God but going beyond the bounds that He has set. Man is like a horse in a lush pasture who jumps the hedge and lands in a quagmire. Man lives within the place of God's green, rich pasture and finds that he wants to get out and leaps the wall, as it were, of God's law and lands in the muck of sin. God has given His law and has written it in the heart of man (Rom. 2:15), and He's revealed it in the Scripture. And because it is "holy, and just, and good" (Rom. 7:12*b*), there is nothing impure, unfair, or evil in it. There is no sane reason to break it, because obedience to it is the path of blessing. But man breaks it, because man seeks to live apart from God's law.

II. WHAT IS SIN LIKE?

Here we go past the definition of sin and look at its nature. We can best see what it's like by examining its characteristics of:

A. Defilement

Not only is sin a defection or a disobedience from God's law, but it is a pollution of that law. It is to the soul what scars are to a lovely face, what stain is to a white silk cloth, or what smog is to an azure blue sky. It makes the soul red with guilt and black with sin—it defiles. In fact, its defiling character is conveyed in the Old Testament in such graphic terms that we can never forget them:

1. Isaiah 30:22—"Ye shall defile also the covering of thy carved images of silver, and the ornament of thy melted images of gold; thou shalt cast them away like an unclean cloth." Isaiah describes sin as an "unclean cloth," which has reference in the Hebrew to the bloody cloth from a woman's menstrual period. That is how God sees the defilement of sin.

2. 1 Kings 8:38—The writer compares the sin of man's heart with sores that come on the body from a deadly plague.

3. Zechariah 3:3—The prophet sees sin as filthy garments on the high priest, Joshua. Over and over again we find in Scripture that sin is seen as something vile, defiling, wretched, and filthy, which pollutes that which is pure.

4. Zechariah 11:8—"My soul loathed them." It is amazing that God should so despise the defilement of sin that He loathes what it does to the sinner.

5. Ezekiel 20:43—Furthermore, Ezekiel says that when the repentant sinner sees his sin, he loathes himself. It is so defiling God hates it, and so does the sinner.

6. 2 Corinthians 7:1—The apostle Paul calls it "filthiness of the flesh and spirit."

So we find that sin is defiling. Second, sin is:

B. Rebellion

1. Leviticus 26:27—God describes those who rebel as people who walk contrary to Him. Sin is defying God. It is walking in opposition or antagonism to Him.

2. Hebrews 10:29—The rebellion of sin can also be described as the sinner trampling on God's law, affronting God by slapping Him in the face, as it were, and spitting on Jesus Christ. Hebrews says that the ones who receive the truth and reject it are those "who hath trodden under foot the son of God, and hath counted the blood of the covenant, with which he was sanctified, an unholy thing." Sin is a flat-out, open, flagrant rebellion.

3. Jeremiah 44:17—One Hebrew word for sin, *pesha,* signifies the rebellion that is in the heart of every man and woman.

Such rebellion is epitomized by the Jews' rejection of Jeremiah's divine message to them: "But we will certainly do whatsoever thing goeth forth out of our own mouth." In other words, "We'll do exactly what we want!"

If sin had its way, it would murder God as it did Jesus Christ. Sin would not only dethrone God, but annul the deity of God. If the sinner had his way, God would cease to be God, and Christ would cease to be Christ.

Third, sin is:

C. Ingratitude

1. Acts 17:28—"For in him we live, and move, and have our being." Do you know that the very fact that you live and exist, you owe to God? Do you know that everybody who's existing in the world today is a creature made by God for a divine purpose and a divine end? God has created you to show forth His praise and to grant glory to Himself. God has a purpose for you that is beyond anything you could imagine. And yet, there are people who live in absolute ingratitude, who spite the very face of Jesus Christ, who mock God, turning their backs on God. But God has created man for His glory, to dwell in an eternal kingdom of bliss with Him, and man not only doesn't want it, but spites the very One who offers it.

2. Matthew 5:45—"For he maketh his sun to rise on the evil and on the good, and sendeth rain on the just and on the unjust." If there's any joy in this life, it's because God gave it to you. If there's any sunshine in life, it's because God put it there. If there's any rain to make your life fresh, it's because God let it fall on you. Everything you are and have is because of God's gracious and marvelous love that is poured out on all men. God isn't responsible for the evil—that's man rebellion. God is responsible for the good. It is God who has provided all the food the sinner eats. God has made a world of color and brightness, and love and music, and all of the things that make life worth living. It is God who has given the senses so that you can enjoy His creation. He has granted beauty for your eye to behold. And it is God who gives intellect and emotions so that you can think, feel, work, play, and rest and your life might be useful. God has given to every individual a special skill and ability to excel in some area. He has created the love and laughter that enables men to care for each other and enjoy one another's fellowship. It is God who providentially preserves us from getting every disease and

dying every death. Though God literally surrounds the sinner with mercy, the sinner says no, and in flagrant, open rebellion to the laws of God, defiles himself and acts in an attitude of ingratitude.

3. 2 Samuel 16:15—17:4—Such ingratitude is illustrated by Absalom, who, after his father, David, had kissed and embraced him, went out and plotted treason against his own father. And so does the sinner indulge himself in God's grace, taking the best that life and love can bring to him and then turns his back on God and walks into the fold of the enemy, Satan. We might ask the same question that is asked in 2 Samuel 16:17, "Is this thy kindness to thy friend?" Essentially, this is the same question that was posed to Judas: "Judas, betrayest thou the Son of man with a kiss?" (Luke 22:48*b*).

God may ask the sinner, "Did I give you life to sin? Did I give you mercy to serve the devil?" Sin is such gross ingratitude, it seeks to dethrone and destroy the source of all that it has received. Even the things the sinners pervert—money, comforts, sexual pleasures, and all other things given by God—they use to bring dishonor to Him.

Fourth, sin is humanly:

D. Incurable

1. Jeremiah 13:23—"Can the Ethiopian change his skin, or the leopard his spots? Then may ye also do good, that are accustomed to do evil." If a leopard can change his spots or an Ethiopian change his skin, then you can make good out of bad. But it can't be done. Sin is an incurable disease. Man does not have the resource to deal with it.

2. Isaiah 1:4-6—"Ah, sinful nation, a people laden with iniquity, a seed of evildoers, children that are corrupters; they have forsaken the Lord, they have provoked the Holy One of Israel unto anger, they are gone away backward. Why should ye be stricken any more? Ye will revolt more and more; the whole head is sick, and the whole heart faint. From the sole of the foot even unto the head there is no soundness in it, but wounds, and bruises, and putrefying sores. They have not been closed, neither bound up, neither mollified with ointment." In other words, man has a horrible, incurable, pervasive disease that cannot be mitigated by human means.

3. Titus 1:15—Paul says that unbelieving man's "conscience is defiled." Man is rotten on the inside. The conscience is given

to man to control his behavior, and if that is defiled, then the resulting actions will be defiled as well.

John Flavel said, "All the tears of a penitent sinner, should he shed as many as there have fallen drops of rain since the creation, cannot wash away sin! The everlasting burnings in hell cannot purify the flaming conscience from the least sin." In other words, he is saying sin is incurable. There is no human cure—not human will, reformation, education, legislation, consultation, counseling, nor self-righteousness. Sin is a disease that is so deep, it can only be cured by the blood of the divine Physician, without which there is no forgiveness of sin (Heb. 9:22).

What is sin like? We have seen that it is defilement, rebellion, ingratitude, and an incurable disease. That brings us to a fifth aspect of sin. It is:

E. Hated by God

Sin is the very antithesis of what God is. It is the only thing God hates. God doesn't resist a man because he's poor—He especially loves the poor. God doesn't resist a man because he's ignorant—He cares for him, too. God does not resist a person because he's crippled—He has made the blind, the deaf, and the lame. God does not resist a man because he's ill, nor because a person is despised by the world. God is antagonistic only to sin.

1. Habakkuk 1:13—"Thou art of purer eyes than to behold evil, and canst not look on iniquity."

2. Jeremiah 44:4—God called out through His prophets with tears and a breaking heart, "Oh, do not this abominable thing that I hate." God hates sin because sin separates man from God, breaking the very thing for which God made man—fellowship.

Sixth, sin is:

F. Hard Work

All it causes is pain, and yet, it amazes me how busy people are doing it. Though it may bring a temporary enjoyment, it ultimately brings grief, death, and hell—but people still work at it.

1. Jeremiah 9:5—Sadly did Jeremiah admit that his people "weary themselves to commit iniquity."

2. Psalm 7:14—"Behold, he travaileth with iniquity." The word "travaileth" is used for birth pains, the most severe kind of

human pain known to them in that day. So, the idea is that the wicked willingly would go through birth pains without an anesthetic to accomplish their evil. In the historical context, this verse probably has reference to an enemy of David, who was chasing him relentlessly.

3. Proverbs 4:16—"For they sleep not, except they have done mischief; and their sleep is taken away, unless they cause some to fall." The wicked don't even go to bed unless they've gotten their evil done. They stay awake figuring out ways to accomplish it (cf. Isa. 5:18).

4. Ezekiel 24:12—"She hath wearied herself with lies."

It's amazing, but people go to hell sweating—they really do. They work hard at being sinners. That's why the Bible says that when you come to Jesus Christ, there is rest: "Come unto me, all ye that labor and are heavy laden, and I will give you rest" (Matt. 11:28). Rest from what? For one thing, from the work that sin is. What a wretched thing! The evil of sin is so wretched that millions of people are damned by its power, and so wretched that it took the very death of Christ Himself to remove it from the life of man.

A third question that we need to answer is:

III. HOW MANY PEOPLE DOES SIN AFFECT?

A. Its Extent

The answer to this is found all through the Bible, but let me just give you a few representative verses:

1. Romans 5:12—"Wherefore, as by one man sin entered into the world, and death by sin, and so death passed upon all men, for all have sinned."

2. Romans 3:23—"For all have sinned, and come short of the glory of God."

3. Romans 3:19—"That every mouth may be stopped, and all the world may become guilty before God."

B. Its Transmission

1. Described

So, we find that sin entered the world through one man. Gentiles don't understand that too well, but the Jewish mind understands it, because Jewish people see themselves not as individuals, but always as a part of a nation, apart from which they have no individual existence.

a) Joshua 7—When Achan sinned, his whole family died, and the whole nation of Israel failed in their next battle. He was acting, in a sense, for a family and even for a nation.

b) Hebrews 7:9-10—Levi paid tithes to Melchizedek in the loins of Abraham, who lived long before Levi was even born.

The Jews have always seen themselves bound up in their ancestry. And so it is, as Paul writes in Romans 5, that when Adam sinned, everybody bound in the loins of Adam that ever issued out of human life became sinful. So Adam's sin is our sin by propagation.

c) Job 14:4—"Who can bring a clean thing out of an unclean? Not one." If you start out with an evil father and mother, you're going to get an evil child.

d) Psalm 58:3—"The wicked are estranged from the womb; they go astray as soon as they are born, speaking lies."

e) Psalm 51:5—"Behold, I was shaped in iniquity, and in sin did my mother conceive me."

And so, not only is the guilt of Adam's sin imputed to us, but the depravity and the corruption of his nature is transmitted to us. The poison goes from the spring to the well to the people that drink. That's what theologians call original sin. You don't come into this world any other way than as a sinner.

2. Debated

Now there once was a big argument about how Adam's sin affected mankind. One theologian, Pelagius, said that when you come into the world, you have a neutral relation to sin and you can choose to be a sinner or not. But another theologian, Augustine, had an answer to that: "Find me one who didn't choose sin, and I might believe it." Needless to say, one could never be found.

3. Decided

When you come into this world, you are a sinner. We've all sinned in Adam, coming short of the glory of God. We have all been born in corruption because we are all Adam's progeny, and as the progeny of Adam, we bear the corruption that he bore.

a) Romans 7:25—"With the flesh, [I serve] the law of sin." Sin is in our nature, woven into the warp and woof of our lives. Adam's sin clings to every man just like Naaman's leprosy clung to Gehazi (2 Kings 5:27). The leprosy of Adam clings to all those who have followed Adam. Nobody is left out. And because the roots of sin are this deep, even when one becomes a Christian the roots of sin are still there. Consequently, we still struggle like Paul, who says in Romans, "For the good that I would, I do not; but the evil which I would not, that I do. . . . But I see another law in my members, warring against the law of my mind, and bringing me into captivity to the law of sin which is in my members" (Rom. 7:19, 23).

b) Hebrews 12:1—"Let us lay aside every weight, and the sin which doth so easily beset us, and let us run with patience the race that is set before us." Why is it so easy for sin to beset us? It's so deep in our nature. We are sinners—no one escapes.

IV. WHAT IS THE RESULT OF SIN?

A. Sin Causes Evil to Overpower Us

1. Evil dominates the mind

   a) Jeremiah 17:9—"The heart is deceitful above all things, and desperately wicked."

   b) Ephesians 4:17-19—"Gentiles walk, in the vanity of their mind, having the understanding darkened, being alienated from the life of God through the ignorance that is in them, because of the blindness of their heart; who, being past feeling, have given themselves over unto lasciviousness." In other words, the minds of unbelievers are dominated by evil.

   c) 1 Corinthians 2:14—"But the natural man receiveth not the things of the Spirit of God; for they are foolishness unto him, neither can he know them, because they are spiritually discerned." The natural man who is separated from God is spiritually dead.

2. Evil dominates the will

   Jeremiah 44:16-17 records the Egyptian Jews' willful rejection of God's messenger: "We will not hearken unto thee. But we will certainly do whatsoever thing goeth forth out of our own mouth." Sin dominates not only how we think, but it dominates that which determines what we do.

3. Evil dominates the affections

    a) 1 John 2:15—"Love not the world, neither the things that are in the world." It's so easy for us to be dominated by sin so that we love the wrong things or love things the wrong way.

    b) John 3:19—"Light is come into the world, and men loved darkness rather than light, because their deeds were evil."

So, sin dominates the affections, the will, and the mind, and ultimately, because man's entire being is dominated by evil, his behavior will be evil. That's the result of original sin, the residual effects of which even the Christian must face. Upon the believer, its effect is like the tree in Daniel 4:23—though the branches and main trunk were cut down, the stump and the roots remained. Similarly, though when a person becomes a Christian a lot of sin is whacked off, the stump is still there until Jesus comes (1 John 3:2). According to John 15, the Father is busy pruning off sin's shoots that keep coming up in our lives as Christians. The Christian must realize as well as the non-Christian that sin is so deep in our nature it's like a sleeping lion and the least thing will awaken its rage. Our sin nature smolders like a fire ready to be ignited, and the slightest wind of temptation fans it into flame. Therefore, if you are an unbeliever, you need to run to Jesus Christ to have it covered, and if you're a Christian, you need to be sure you don't do anything to induce it to wake from its sleep. So, though sin overpowers us, it is a power that can be broken by Christ.

B. Sin Brings Us Under the Control of Satan

Who would ever choose to be dominated by that evil being? And yet the Bible says that those who don't know Jesus Christ have done that very thing.

1. Ephesians 2:2—"In which in times past ye walked according to the course of this world, according to the prince of the power of the air, the spirit that now worketh in the sons of disobedience." If you don't know Jesus Christ, Satan is at work in your life.

2. John 8:44—Jesus said to the hypocritical Pharisees, "Ye are of your father the devil."

3. 1 John 5:19—"The whole world lieth in wickedness [lit., 'the wicked one']."

4. Romans 6:16—Paul says that apart from God man is a servant of sin and, by implication, ultimately Satan.

And so, what is the effect of sin in our lives? First of all, it overpowers us, so that our thinking, feelings, will, and behavior are dominated by it. Second, it brings us under the dominion of the evil adversary Satan, where there is no freedom—only slavery.

How to Be Free from the Power of Satan

Satan can make a man think he is free when he really isn't. But when somebody comes to trust in Jesus Christ, he finds true freedom. Jesus said in John 8:36, "If the Son, therefore, shall make you free, ye shall be free indeed." Why did He say that? Because Satan sells a phony freedom.

How many movements can you think of today that are called "liberation movements"? Is man really free? Not on your life! He is in bondage to sin. It is only the Lord Jesus Christ who can free him. That's why Paul described his divinely given mission of preaching the gospel of Christ as one designed "to open their [the Gentiles'] eyes, and to turn them from darkness to light, and from the power of Satan unto God, that they may receive forgiveness of sins, and inheritance" (Acts 26:18a).

C. Sin Makes Us the Objects of God's Wrath

1. Ephesians 2:3—Paul identifies those controlled by their sin nature as "children of wrath," a bull's eye for God's judgment.

2. Psalm 90:11—Moses said, "Who knoweth the power of thine anger? Even according to thy fear, so is thy wrath." Who can measure God's almighty wrath? By the way, God's wrath is not just a passion. God's wrath is an act of His pure and holy will against sin which defiles His universe. You have to ask yourself when you read the Bible and you read about God's wrath, how sinners can go on blindly in their sin.

3. Galatians 3:10-11—"Cursed is everyone that continueth not in all things which are written in the book of the law, to do them. But that no man is justified by the law in the sight of God, it is evident; for, The just shall live by faith." If you don't come to God through faith, you will be cursed.

4. 1 Corinthians 16:22—"If any man love not the Lord Jesus Christ, let him be Anathema [accursed]."

God is very serious about how sin overpowers us, controls us, and makes us objects of His wrath. I don't know how a sinner can eat, drink, and be merry if he knows that's a fact. Such a response is illustrated by the story of Damocles, who sat **eating** at a banquet while a sword hung over his head by a small thread, and yet he still had the stomach to eat. In like manner, the sword of God's wrath hangs over the head of the sinner, and yet he goes on eating, drinking, and making merry. Only Christ can save us from "the wrath to come," as 1 Thessalonians 1:10 tells us. Aren't you glad that if you're a Christian, you've been delivered from the wrath to come?

D. Sin Subjects Us to the Miseries of Life

When you follow the path of sin, you go from one misery to another, as the following verses show.

1. Job 5:7—"Yet man is born unto trouble."

2. Romans 8:20—Paul says that "the creation was made subject to vanity." In other words, creation has been temporarily subjected to a degree of uselessness or emptiness.

3. Ecclesiastes 1:2—Solomon recognized that something was missing in life that could not satisfy the heart. "Vanity of vanities, saith the Preacher, vanity of vanities; all is vanity." Solomon looked at everything and concluded that it all meant nothing. He tried it all, and all it produced was emptiness, bitterness, sorrow, meaninglessness, and uselessness.

4. Genesis 49:4—Sin degrades man of his honor. Because of incest, Reuben lost his dignity.

5. Isaiah 48:22—"There is no peace, saith the Lord, unto the wicked." Sin has robbed man of peace. He has become like the troubled sea when it cannot rest, whose waters churn up mire and dirt.

Judas was so vile and evil that he followed the path of trouble until finally, in absolute horror and desperation with a conscience that was shouting so loud he couldn't stand to hear it, he took a rope, tied it around his neck, and hanged himself. His rope broke, and his body was crushed on the rocks below in his attempt to escape his conscience. All he accomplished was to wind up in hell where his conscience will be louder in eternity than he ever heard it before.

A fifth result of sin is that:

E. Sin Damns the Soul to Hell

People think they can sin and get away with it, but they can't. This assumption was amply illustrated in a newspaper article about a man who died after arriving at Los Angeles International Airport. An autopsy revealed that he had half a million dollars worth of cocaine packed in eleven rubber containers in his stomach. The coroner said that one or more of the containers appeared to have leaked, causing the individual to die of an overdose of the drug. Sin is that way—you may think you can contain a lot of it in your life, but it will eventually leak out and kill you.

To see that sin damns the soul to hell, all you have to do is read Revelation 20 about the great white throne judgment and how people are cast into the lake of fire. And did you realize that over 50 million people die every year, which means 136,986 die every day, 5,707 every hour, and 95 every minute? Furthermore, there are 4.25 billion people in the world who will all die sooner or later and are being replaced at two and one-half times the death rate. So not only are people all dying, but more of them are being born to die all the time. Hell is waiting for its victims.

Henry Van Dyke said, "Remember that what you possess in this world will be found at the day of your death and belong to someone else; what you are will be yours forever." Sin will damn a soul. I don't especially like to talk about hell, but Jesus talked more about it than anybody else in the whole Bible. Spurgeon said, "Many of you are hanging over the mouth of hell by a solitary plank and that plank is rotten." And so we see the deadly evil of sin.

We've answered some questions about sin: What is it? What is it like? How many does it affect? And what are its results? But there is a fifth and final question, which is most helpful:

V. WHAT DO WE DO ABOUT SIN?

A. The Principles

1. Romans 6:23—"For the wages of sin is death, but the gift of God is eternal life through Jesus Christ, our Lord." That's the key, isn't it? When Jesus died on the cross He paid the penalty for your sin, and He offers you forgiveness.

2. Romans 4:7-8—"Blessed are they whose iniquities are forgiven, and whose sins are covered. Blessed is the man to whom the Lord will not impute sin." In other words, happy is the man who knows that God has forgiven all his sin and covered it with righteousness. Happy is the man who knows that God will never charge sin to his account. Happy is the man who knows the debt is canceled and the price is paid. Happy is the man who comes to Jesus Christ and takes the free gift. That's true happiness.

B. The Practice

As a Christian, if there is the slightest taint of indifference toward sin and the victory Christ offers over it, then you have lost some of the sense of gratitude that you ought to have in your heart for what God has done for you. I hope by acknowledging again the seriousness of sin, you regain a spirit of gratefulness for having been forgiven.

You may say, "I've come to Jesus Christ. Now, how do I deal with sin in my life?" The answer is simple: First:

1. Recognize your sin has been forgiven

   John reminded his readers, "I write unto you, little children, because your sins are forgiven you for his name's sake" (1 John 2:12).

2. Recognize you have the power to say no

   Paul exhorts us in Colossians 3:5 to "mortify" the deeds of the body. You say, "John, how do you say no to sin?" By saying yes to God. Sin will fight against that which you know is righteous. But, depending upon whether it is sin or the Spirit of God who dominates your life, you will say yes to one or the other.

What does a man or woman do about sin? They come to Jesus Christ so that it can be forgiven. Then, as believers, when we face temptations and sin, we can stand on the confidence that it's already been forgiven. We don't need to get into some emotional guilt trip. And then we move to the strength provided for us in the power of the Spirit of God, the Word of God. We must become so saturated with the Word that it dominates our thinking, and when the temptation comes we react in accordance to the righteousness of the Word, rather than to sin.

Focusing on the Facts

1. Why is it dangerous to tone down the seriousness of sin (see p. 80)?
2. What must God do before paradise is to be regained (see pp. 80-81)?
3. Name the three relationships that sin destroys (see p. 81).
4. Who has the virus of sin and is captured in its power? Who did it not capture (see p. 81)?
5. What is the primary definition of sin, and on what verse is it based (see p. 83)?
6. What is the path of blessing with regard to God's law (see p. 83)?
7. Match the specific character of sin with those who emphasized that aspect (see p. 84).

A. Defilement	1. Rejecting Jeremiah (Jer. 44:17)
B. Rebellion	2. David embracing Absalom, who plots treason (2 Sam. 16:15—17:4)
C. Ingratitude	3. Those who don't sleep unless they cause some to fall (Prov. 4:16)
D. Incurable	4. Filthy garments on the high priest (Zech. 3:3)
E. Hated by God	5. The Ethiopian is unable to change his skin (Jer. 13:23)
F. Hard Work	6. A holy God cannot look upon iniquity (Hab. 1:13)

8. Why was the conscience given to man? What will the results be if it becomes defiled (see pp. 86-87)?
9. What is the only thing that God hates (see p. 87)?
10. What is the extent of sin's effect upon man? Cite one verse to support your answer (see pp. 88-89).
11. Whose guilt and depravity is transmitted to all mankind? What do theologians call this (see p. 89)?
12. What is the only status that a man has when he is born into the world (see p. 89)?
13. Why is it so easy for sin to "beset us" (Heb. 12:1; see p. 90)?
14. Why does "the natural man" (1 Cor. 2:14) separated from God not understand spiritual things (see p. 90)?
15. What does 1 John 2:15 identify as that which can easily dominate our affections (see p. 91)?
16. As Paul talks to the Ephesian Christians in Ephesians 2:2, when does he say that they were under the control of Satan (see p. 91)?
17. As he preached the gospel Paul was commissioned to turn man from what two things (Acts 26:18; see p. 92)?
18. How can a man escape "the wrath to come," according to 1 Thessalonians 1:10 (see p. 93)?
19. What did Solomon conclude about life when it is lived for oneself apart from the plan of God (see p. 93)?
20. Though people may think they can get away with sin, where does Revelation 20:11-15 say that sin will ultimately lead them (see p. 94)?
21. According to Romans 4:7-8 and Psalm 32:1-2, who is the one who is blessed or happy (see p. 94)?

Pondering the Principles

1. Have you been guilty of ingratitude for any of the things God has done for you? When was the last time you thanked Him for forgiving your sins? Do you remember some times that He saved you from some devastating consequences of your sin? Sit down with your family or friends and take turns thanking God for all He has given

you and all He has done for you. Read together Luke 17:11-19, discussing the following questions: How many of the lepers were healed physically? How many were healed spiritually? Which of the lepers exhibited true saving faith? Why do you think so? Who received the greater blessing? What will God's response be to those who honor him (1 Sam. 2:30)?

2. Because sin causes evil to overpower all men, though not to the same degree, what advice would you give to a non-Christian who wanted to take the first step to combat the sin problem? To a Christian who found it easy to fall into sin? Of these two verses, Romans 6:22-23 or Romans 13:14, which would be the most applicable to the Christian who is easily tempted?

3. We must become so saturated with the Word of God that it dominates our thinking so that when temptation comes, we react in accordance to the righteousness of the Word, rather than to sin. Note Luke 4:1-13 to see how Jesus faced temptation. When temptation arises, do you find yourself thinking of how to get away with sinning, or thinking about which scripture most accurately instructs you how to respond to the situation? If your response is not the latter one, then maybe you should make a commitment to spending more time in the Word, reading, studying, and teaching it at your family, neighborhood, church, or co-workers' Bible study.

6

The Simple Gospel

Outline

Introduction
A. The Choice of Rejection
   1. Matthew 12:30
   2. Deuteronomy 30:19-20
   3. Joshua 24:15
   4. John 3:18
   5. Revelation 22:17
   6. John 5:39-40
   7. Romans 1:20
   8. John 16:8-9
   9. Revelation 2:21
B. The Context of Rejection
   1. The evidence revealed
   2. The evidence rejected
C. The Consequences of Rejection
   1. Dying in depravity
   2. Removal of revelation
      a) Amos 8:11-12
      b) Proverbs 1:24-31
D. The Character of Rejection
   1. The supreme sin
   2. The substituted salvation
   3. The superficial search
      a) Romans 10:2
      b) Jeremiah 29:13

Lesson
I. Be Self-Righteous
A. The Assumption of the Jews
   1. Identified
   2. Illustrated
B. The Answer of Jesus
II. Be Earthbound
A. Worldliness Defined

Introduction

It's wonderful when people come to Christ—they no longer are under the tyranny of sin and guilt or of lust and desire, and they no longer are under the bondage of a purposeless and meaningless kind of existence. Christ not only gives meaning to life, but He restores harmony to our spiritual lives by completely forgiving our sin.

Now, what happens when somebody does not want to establish a relationship with the living God through Jesus Christ? What happens when a person maintains the masquerade of Christmas, giving homage to an event but not tolerating the individual in which that event finds its meaning? If receiving Jesus Christ results in an abundant and eternal life, then *not* receiving Jesus Christ results in receiving the curse of God.

As we find in this passage of John 8 some very alarming statements by Jesus, I must admit they make the passage a difficult thing for me to discuss, let alone understand. I sometimes want to cry out with Richard Baxter, "Oh, for an empty hell and a full heaven!" It is not my desire, nor is it Jesus' desire, for anyone to enter hell, for God is "not willing that any should perish, but that all should come to repentance" (2 Pet. 3:9*b*). It is not condemnation, but rather warning, that Jesus speaks in these verses.

A. The Choice of Rejection

It ought to be brought to our attention that people who give lip service to Christianity while rejecting Christ are engaged in the most foolish kind of fun. It would be comparable to people having a party on the *Lusitania* as they went on ignoring the

99

reality of the German threat. If people really knew that their eternal destiny was determined by the Christ of Christmas, whom they in actuality rejected, I doubt whether there would be much for them to celebrate.

All throughout the Bible it is made clear that there is no neutrality on this issue:

1. Matthew 12:30—Jesus put it simply and succinctly when He said, "He that is not with me is against me."

2. Deuteronomy 30:19-20—All the way back into the first set of writings that the Bible gives us, the Pentateuch, Moses establishes the pattern that continues all the way to the book of Revelation: "I call heaven and earth to record this day against you, that I have set before you life and death, blessing and cursing; therefore, choose." Here are the same two things that we see right through Scripture—life or death, blessing or cursing.

3. Joshua 24:15—"Choose you this day whom ye will serve, whether the gods which your fathers served that were on the side of the river, or the gods of the Amorites, in whose land ye dwell; but as for me and my house, we will serve the Lord." Two options are given—serving the true God or serving false gods.

4. John 3:18—"He that believeth on him is not condemned; but he that believeth not is condemned already." You only have two choices—you're either condemned to hell or not condemned. And the crux of the issue is whether you believe. Then the reason for condemnation is given at the end of the verse: "Because he hath not believed in the name of the only begotten Son of God."

5. Revelation 22:17—This book closes with an invitation: "And the Spirit and the bride say, Come. And let him that heareth say, Come. And let him that is athirst come. And whosoever will, let him take the water of life freely." There again is the choice of one of two ways.

The other day one of my children asked me, "Daddy, is it true that there are only two places you can go when you die, heaven or hell?" And I said, "That's true, only two—heaven or hell." There is no neutral ground, no purgatory, no waiting place in this day and age. Hell may have different designations as to its final form and identity, but there are only two places—heaven, where God is, or hell, where God is not. You may have heard the old line "He had nobody to blame but himself." That is actually biblical. There may be a big theological argument about who is responsible when people get saved—whether it's God, or whether men have anything to do with it—but there's no question about who is responsible in the Bible when people go to hell, because it says that men choose.

6. John 5:39-40—Jesus substantiated the reality of man's choice of hell when he confronted some of the Jews, saying, "Search the scriptures; for in them ye think ye have eternal life; and they are they which testify of me. And ye will not come to me, that ye might have life." The responsibility belongs to us.

7. Romans 1:20—Realizing that man is responsible for his choices, Paul says that men "are without excuse."

8. John 16:8-9—"And when he [the Holy Spirit] is come, he will reprove the world of sin . . . because they believe not on me." To not believe on Christ is the sin of all sins.

9. Revelation 2:21—The Lord condemns Jezebel, who was misleading the church at Thyatira, saying, "And I gave her space to repent of her fornication, and she repented not." In other words, God has given the call to repentance, and when people do not repent and turn to Him in faith, that is their own fault, for they are responsible.

B. The Context of Rejection

Now as we come to John 8, we notice in verse 21 a powerful statement on the part of Jesus given to the Jewish leaders: "Then said Jesus again unto them, I go my way, and ye shall seek me, and shall die in your sins [or 'sin']; where I go, ye cannot come." Here Jesus is making a very strong statement about the fact that He is going to heaven and they are not.

1. The evidence revealed

Already by chapter 8 He can give such a warning, because they have had enough information to have made a decision about Him. For eight chapters, John has been chronicling the self-manifestation of God in Christ by recording the many wonders He had accomplished in Galilee and in Jerusalem. Furthermore, Jesus has said many astounding things. His claims to deity are clear—nobody need mistake them. In fact, later on Jesus exhorts those Jews who were evaluating His ministry that they should believe Him for the words and the works that He had said and done (John 10:37-38; 14:10-11).

Through the chapters, we see His works and hear His words again and again. In chapter 1, He is introduced by John as God incarnate, who "was made flesh, and dwelt among us . . . the only begotten of the Father" (v. 14). In John 2, He performs His first miracle at Cana as He changes water into wine. In John 4, we see Him reveal a woman's personal life, never having known her, and talk about the fact that He is living water. In John 5, we hear His dialogue with the Pharisees as He claims to be God, who has been commissioned by His Father to make all ultimate judgment. In John 6, we see Him doing many miracles all day long, including feeding the thousands of people on a hillside in Galilee. In John 7, He proceeds to Jerusalem, and the things that He says there continue to support that He is God. In John 8, He forgives sin and claims to be the light of the world. All of these words and works, and signs and wonders, should have been sufficient to elicit genuine faith and confidence in who He was. And in the mind of Jesus, anyone who was seeing, hearing, and experiencing those things, yet not believing, bears alone the guilt of their own sin—they are without excuse.

2. The evidence rejected

Even though many had their physical needs met by Jesus Christ, they still rejected Him, not wanting to have to face the spiritual need for repentance and belief in Him. In Galilee, big crowds initially followed Him because He fed and healed them. But when He started laying down some principles of life and meddling in their sin, they stopped wanting to crown Him king. When He came to Jerusalem, the same thing happened. Great crowds followed Him everywhere. But as He began to turn away from the physical to the spiritual and deal with the sin in the hearts of people, the crowds began to melt away, until finally the only crowd left was a group of Pharisees trying to figure out how to kill Him. Such a tragic rejection was epitomized in John's words: "He came unto his own, and his own received him not" (John 1:11). The Jews were responsible for their conclusions about Christ, as are you and I and every other person.

Though some did believe, John 7:40-41 tells us there were others who didn't: "Many of the people, therefore, when they heard this saying, said, Of a truth this is the Prophet. Others said, This is the Christ. But some said, Shall Christ come out of Galilee?" To some who rejected Him Jesus said, "And ye will not come to me, that ye might have life" (John 5:40). But they had nobody to blame but themselves, as do all who have full revelation, and yet turn away from the truth (Heb. 6, 10).

C. The Consequences of Rejection

Though the unbelief of the scribes and Pharisees was manifested in their desire to kill Jesus, verse 20 says that "no man laid hands on him; for his hour was not yet come." Being held back by God from being able to take His life at this point, they are confronted by Jesus in verse 21: "I go my way, and ye shall seek me, and shall die in your [sin]; where I go, ye cannot come."

1. Dying in depravity

This confrontation reveals the tragic result of refusing Jesus Christ—dying in one's sin. Jesus hints at this in the previous chapter when He says, "Yet a little while am I with you, and then I go unto him that sent me. Ye shall seek me, and shall not find me; and where I am, there ye cannot come. Then said the Jews among themselves, Where will he go, that we shall not find him? Will he go unto the dispersed among the Greeks, and teach the Greeks?" (John 7:33-35).

Whereas they are honestly confused about what He means in chapter 7, in chapter 8 the Jews become cynical when Jesus repeats essentially the same warning: "Then said the Jews, Will he kill himself?" (John 8:22). But their cynicism only serves to reveal their lack of understanding. Jesus was simply saying that He was going to go to the Father in heaven and that they would be unable to join Him, because they would be in hell, having rejected Him. If they sought Him too late, their seeking would be in vain.

2. Removal of revelation

There is a limit to the grace God will bestow upon those who reject Him.

a) Amos 8:11-12—"Behold, the days come, saith the Lord God, that I will send a famine in the land, not a famine of bread, nor a thirst for water, but of hearing the words of the Lord; and they shall wander from sea to sea, and from the north even to the east; they shall run to and fro to seek the word of the Lord, and shall not find it." And the same thing is true of His gospel about Christ.

b) Proverbs 1:24-31—Divine wisdom is personified, turning away from those who would reject it. "Because I have called, and ye refused; I have stretched out my hand, and no man regarded, but ye have set at nought all my coun-

103

sel, and would have none of my reproof, I also will laugh at your calamity; I will mock when your fear cometh; when your fear cometh as desolation, and your destruction cometh as a whirlwind; when distress and anguish come upon you. Then shall they call upon me, but I will not answer; they shall seek me early, but they shall not find me; because they hated knowledge, and did not choose the fear of the Lord. They would have none of my counsel; they despised all my reproof. Therefore shall they eat of the fruit of their own way, and be filled with their own devices." In other words, when the day of grace has ended, those who have rejected God's wisdom will be responsible and will pay the consequences that they themselves have earned. It is like the prisoner who was instructed by the king to make a chain. Every day he added another link, until finally, they took him and bound him with his own chain. That is how it is with sinful people who reject Christ. They are producing by their life their own ultimate disaster.

D. The Character of Rejection

Whereas Jesus' death would take Him to the Father, the death of those who rejected Him would not, because of sin. Now what sin did Jesus have in mind when He told the Pharisees that they would die in their sin?

1. The supreme sin

This is the sin of rejecting Christ. John 16:8-9 says that the Holy Spirit will convict of sin, because they did not believe in Christ. If you want to rationalize and say, "Well, I don't commit any sins; I'm a very good person, and I try to do everything I can," it will be of no avail, because if you have never received Jesus Christ, that is the ultimate sin. This is why Jesus says that those who do not seek Him will die with sin that is unforgiven. Of course that is the supreme disaster, because such a person is destined for hell.

2. The substituted salvation

Those Jewish leaders did seek heaven all their lives long. But do you want to know something? They sought it in the wrong place. Instead of seeking it at the feet of Jesus, they sought it in their own self-righteousness. Romans 10:17 says that faith comes by hearing a message about Christ. But instead of seeking it there, they sought it in their own books, laws, and rituals.

3. The superficial search

They not only sought it in the wrong place, but they sought it in the wrong way.

a) Romans 10:2—Paul says about the Jews, "For I bear them witness that they have a zeal for God, but not according to knowledge." They were seeking God according to their own system, and it was far from being a whole-hearted search.

b) Jeremiah 29:13—"And ye shall seek me, and find me, when ye shall search for me with all your heart." The scribes and Pharisees didn't give their whole heart to seeking God, because they had devoted their whole heart to the proud propagation of their own self-righteousness.

So, many of the Jews were seeking in the wrong place, in the wrong way, and unfortunately, they would also be found seeking at the wrong time. I'm sure there have been countless people who, when it was far too late, started their search for heaven after sentence had been passed on them for their continual rejection.

I read somewhere that somebody had calculated that at least one hundred people a minute go to hell. That's a fearful thought, isn't it? Jesus tried to convey the fearfulness of hell with some of His parables. For instance, in Matthew 13:40, Jesus says, "As, therefore, the tares are gathered and burned in the fire, so shall it be in the end of this age. The Son of man shall send forth his angels, and they shall gather out of his kingdom all things that offend, and them who do iniquity, and shall cast them into a furnace of fire; there shall be wailing and gnashing of teeth. Then shall the righteous shine forth as the sun in the kingdom of their Father. Who hath ears to hear, let him hear." There are only two places to spend eternity—hell, where there is weeping and gnashing of teeth, or heaven, where you shine as the sun. And Jesus says that if you have ears, then you had better listen. It's a fearful warning.

Why does God warn man?

When Jesus warns the Jews in this passage, He is not brutalizing them by sovereignly ending their choice or putting an end to all possibility. He is merely warning them of the consequence of their present choice. When you hear people criticize God for speaking negatively like this, saying that God is not a loving God, don't believe it for a minute. God is so merciful and so loving that He warns us. No one ever went to hell who didn't choose to go there. But God isn't going to force Himself eternally on someone who doesn't want Him.

Now, there are four elements that I see in the rest of this text that guarantee a person he can die in his sin. Let's look at them.

Lesson

I. BE SELF-RIGHTEOUS (vv. 22-23a)

The first way to guarantee that you will die in your sin and not go to the Father's house in heaven is to be convinced that you don't need to be saved—that you are spiritually all right. By far, those who deny their need of a Savior are the most difficult kind of people to reach. People who claim to be already righteous apart from Christ by saying, "I belong to this special group," or, "I'm one of the 144,000," or, "I've got my papers that say I'm a righteous person," are only deceiving themselves. Self-righteous people, who have developed a system that they believe gives them the right to enter God's presence, are the hardest people to convince that they need a Savior, because they already feel they are all right. Satan is clever. When he puts together a phony system based on human achievement and works-righteousness, he does it in such a complex and supposedly biblical way that it is tremendously deceiving. People become captivated in cults and falsely assume that they can gain righteousness by what they do. But nobody ever comes to Christ who doesn't see Him as a Savior who takes away sin, and himself as a sinner who needs his sin taken away.

A. The Assumption of the Jews (v. 22)

The Jews that Jesus confronts are clearly self-righteous, as you can tell from their answer. Jesus had just given them a loving warning, and their response is a mocking joke: "Then said the Jews, Will he kill himself? because he saith, Where I go, ye cannot come." They implied that Jesus was going to commit suicide.

1. Identified

Now, the Jews believed that suicide was the worst sin, for which the blackest part of Hades was reserved. People who had killed themselves had no possibility of ever entering "Abraham's bosom" (Luke 16:22). Therefore, the Jews concluded that if Jesus killed Himself, He would be going to Hades, the opposite of the place they assumed that they were going. They didn't even understand what Jesus was really saying. They were so self-righteous, having systematized their religion so carefully, that they believed they were the ones who would populate heaven. Nevertheless, Jesus mercifully warns them with an announcement of impending doom. How deaf could they be! If you read the whole New Testament, you would be hard pressed to find a story of the conversion of a Pharisee. There are a few, but not many, because they were such hard people to reach with biblical truth.

The Jews were correct in concluding that Jesus was going to die. However, they were completely wrong in thinking that His death was going to be by suicide. Rather, it was going to be a self-sacrificial, voluntary offering of Himself to be crucified. Acts 2:23 says, "Him, being delivered by the determinate counsel and foreknowledge of God, ye have taken, and by wicked hands have crucified and slain." It was murder, not suicide. But He was a willing victim to accomplish redemption.

Satan's Big Lie

Self-righteousness is the big lie of Satan. The truth is you are saved by Christ; the lie is you are saved by anything other than Christ. That lie can come in all kinds of packages. You can be saved by following these rules, doing these routines, belonging to this or that system, being good enough to outweigh your shortcomings—there are myriad possible systems to counter the one truth, and they are all part of Satan's big lie. If Satan can get somebody into a system that says he is righteous, it's very hard to extract him from it. One reason is that self-righteousness is very proud. I am reminded of what Job said to those who judged him: "No doubt but ye are the people, and wisdom shall die with you" (12:2). Proverbs 12:15 says, "The way of a fool is right in his own eyes." Luke 16:15 says, "That which is highly esteemed among men is abomination in the sight of God." When men believe Satan's lie and develop a system that is highly esteemed in their eyes, it is an abomination to God. Salvation can never be earned by good works and keeping religious rituals.

2. Illustrated

So, the first way to die in your sins is to be self-righteous and laugh at anybody that talks about sin or hell. The world does that all the time. It mocks Jesus, making a joke out of His warnings about hell. It gets no more serious about hell than

107

to put devil suits on little children at Halloween. It refuses to admit its sin and its need of Christ's forgiveness as it trusts in good works or self-made religion for salvation. A person who gets wrapped up into the kind of self-righteous systems that the world offers, whether it is a religious institution like Mormonism or Jehovah's Witnesses or one's self-made system, can become very belligerent once they become committed to it. For example, I read an article that was sent to a Melbourne paper by a person after he had heard Billy Graham preach, which said:

"After hearing Dr. Billy Graham on the air, viewing him on television, and seeing reports and letters concerning his mission, I am heartily sick of the type of religion that insists my soul and everyone else's needs saving, whatever that means. I have never felt that I was lost nor do I feel that I daily wallow in the mire of sin, although repetitious preaching insists that I do. Give me a practical religion that teaches gentleness and tolerance, that acknowledges no barriers of color or creed, that remembers the aged and teaches children goodness and not sin. If in order to save my soul I must accept such a philosophy as I have recently heard preached, I prefer to remain forever damned."

Now that's a pretty precarious position to be in. Evidently, the man has developed a system in which he believes he has attained self-righteousness before God, and therefore fearlessly mocks the truth.

B. The Answer of Jesus (v. 23*a*)

That article exactly reflects the attitude of the Pharisees and scribes. Desiring to give a correct analysis of the situation, Jesus responds to their mockery: "And he said unto them, Ye are from beneath; I am from above." Jesus understood their implication that He was going to kill Himself and go to Hades. But Jesus said, in effect, "It is you who are from Hades; I am from above. You've got it reversed." With this cutting reply, Jesus does not mean that they were literally from Hades; He means that their unbelief, hypocrisy, false religion, ignorance, and willful self-righteousness were spawned from the enemy. He makes the distinction clear that they are following Satan while He is following God. They were—like all unbelieving people are in this world—from beneath in the sense that they were part of the evil system. In John 8:44, Jesus says to them, "Ye are of your father the devil." Such people operate their lives "according to the course of this world, according to the prince of the power of the air" (Eph. 2:2*b*).

Whereas the unbeliever is unknowingly guided by Satan from beneath, the believer is guided from above because his citizenship is in heaven (Phil. 3:20), and he positionally resides "in heavenly places" (Eph. 1:3; 2:6). We are connected to either heaven or hell while we are alive by virtue of who we identify with. So Jesus, warning the Pharisees, puts things in perspective, saying, "Your roots run downward to Hades, because your lifestyle makes it manifest. You had better recognize the source of your religious system." If you want to die in your sin, just follow the Pharisees' attitude—believe you don't need Christ as your Savior, assuming that you are OK, have solved all your problems, and have attained righteousness. Convince yourself of that, and you will die in your sin.

There's a second way to die in your sin, and that is:

II. BE EARTHBOUND (v. 23*b*)

"I am from above: ye are of this world; I am not of this world."

A. Worldliness Defined

Jesus draws another contrast. He tells the Pharisees that they are part of the world system of which He is not. The term "world" simply refers to the invisible spiritual realm of evil. We use the word ourselves to identify a particular system, such as the world of politics, the world of sports, and so on. The system that Jesus has in mind here is the system of evil that is opposed to God and Christ. If you want to guarantee that you will die in your sin, just be a part of the world system, accepting whatever it is offering. Then you can be classified as "children of this world" (Luke 16:8) entrapped in "this present evil world" from which Jesus seeks to deliver man (Gal. 1:4). Opposed to the truth of God, the world propagates its own self-righteous systems.

B. Worldliness Described

You could characterize the system in this way: it is materialistic and humanistic, believing that man is going to solve his problems by himself and rule his own fate; it is lost in preoccupation with sex; it is plagued by carnal ambition, pride, greed, jealousy, envy, self-pleasure and selfish desire, murder, and so on. Its opinions are wrong, its aims are selfish, its pleasures are sinful, its influences are demoralizing, its politics are corrupt, its honors are empty, its smiles are phony, and its love is fickle. Furthermore, it is in the process of dissolution. According to 1 John 2:17, "The world passeth away." It will self-destruct.

So Jesus identifies those mocking Him as being of the world system. They were sinful, selfish, and earthbound souls who were controlled by the dictates of the evil system run by Satan. They had separated themselves from Jesus Christ with a gulf that was impassible. And even though they were religious, and maybe even humanitarian at heart, they were still part of Satan's evil system, opposed to God. Jesus is simply saying to them, "You're going to die in your sins for two reasons—number one, you are self-righteous, and number two, you are totally engulfed in the system. You buy whatever the world is selling."

There's a third way to die in your sins:

III. BE UNBELIEVING (v. 24)

"I said, therefore, unto you, that ye shall die in your sins; for if ye believe not that I am he, ye shall die in your sins."

The third way to guarantee that you will die in your sins is to be unbelieving of the gospel. You don't have to go out and kill somebody and be bad to go to hell, because hell is not just for criminals, it is for everybody and anybody who refuses Christ. If you refuse Christ in this life, God isn't going to force you to dwell with Him forever in eternity. But the way of faith is open—you can believe. Or you can decide not to believe—the choice is yours.

A. The Content of Belief (v. 24a)

You say, "Well, what am I supposed to believe?" I remember a song that used to be popular called "I Believe," which kept on repeating the words "I believe." I believe what? Another song is "I Believe in Music." Well, if that is all you believe in, you are in trouble. You find the same kind of vague or misdirected faith when you ask people, "Do you believe in Christ?" "Yeah, I believe in Christ, He lived and so forth."

But Jesus had something more definite in mind. Notice what He says: "If ye believe not that I am he." In other words, "If you do not believe that I am the One I claim to be." It isn't enough to believe that Jesus is the One that you think He is; you must believe that He is the One He claimed to be. He claimed to be God by such phrases as "I am the bread of life" (John 6:35a), "he that believeth on me shall never thirst" (John 6:35b), "I am the light of the world" (John 8:12b), "I am the good shepherd" (John 10:11a), "I am the door" (John 10:9a), "I am the resurrection, and the life" (John 11:25a), "I am the way, the truth, and the life" (John 14:6a). Therefore, because Jesus was identifying Himself with God, saving faith not only becomes a question of turning from sin, but trusting the Son as well. It's a question of

110

believing Jesus is who He claimed to be. You ask, "Well then, am I going to die in my sin unless I believe that He is all that He claimed to be?" That's right. You ought to find out who He claimed to be, for Romans 10:17 says faith comes by hearing a message about Christ. You can never have true faith unless you hear the truth about Christ. (Some of the old translations say, "Faith cometh by hearing, and hearing by the word of God." But the best Greek manuscripts say, "By the word of Christ.") True faith is the result of hearing and believing with your heart that Jesus is who He claimed to be and that God verified that claim by raising Him from the dead (Rom. 10:9).

B. The Consequence of Unbelief (v. 24b)

Jesus promises His opponents that they will die with their sin unforgiven if they do not believe that He is who He claims to be—God in human flesh. For not to believe and turn away shatters hope and leaves only hell's gloomy foreboding. That's how it is.

One time when I was sitting on a plane, I had a man ask me, "How do you become a Christian?" after he found out that I was a Bible teacher. So I shared the gospel with him, telling him that he must believe that Jesus is who He claimed to be—God in human flesh, the Savior who died for man's sin and rose again. A person can go to hell and remain there eternally for not believing just those few things. Faith in Christ comes by hearing a message about Him, and if you haven't heard enough, then you ought to read some more or find somebody who can tell you more. There is no sense in going to hell for something you failed to do, because not believing is the same thing as rejecting. "He that is not with me is against me" (Matt. 12:30). Don't be like the Pharisees who should have known, but continued to mock.

Finally, we come to the fourth way to die in your sins:

IV. BE WILLFULLY IGNORANT (vv. 25-29)

When someone hears a speech about Christ, but doesn't let it register, that person is willfully ignorant. The Jewish leaders had enough evidence about Christ—they just refused to believe, and in their chosen ignorance, even mocked Him. They were willfully ignorant:

A. Of Christ's Identity (v. 25a)

"Then said they unto him, Who art thou?"

Far from being an honest question, this could be paraphrased, "Who do you think you are, fella? These are some pretty ridiculous things you are saying, telling us that we're going to die in our sin. Do you know who you're talking to? We're the spiritual elite. Who do you think you are? You're some nobody from Nazareth, who has come down here to tell the leaders of Jerusalem how to run things. What gives you the right to assume the role of equality with God?" Such willful ignorance is manifested in other places in Scripture.

1. John 8:19—"Then said they unto him, Where is thy Father? Jesus answered, Ye neither know me, nor my father." "You are hopelessly ignorant. You think you know God, but you really don't. And you think that I'm a fake, so you don't know Me either. You can't recognize the truth because you are so dominated by sin."

2. John 9:30—Do you remember when the blind man was healed in John 9 and all the Jewish leaders wondered how the blind man was able to see, admitting their disbelief in Jesus' power? "The man answered, and said unto them, Why here is a marvelous thing, that ye know not from where he is, and yet he hath opened mine eyes." This blind man had more sense than those Jewish leaders. Why? Because they willed to be ignorant of the truth. Hell will be filled with people who are there simply because they willed to be ignorant, not wanting Jesus to make claims on their lives. They will be those who didn't want to know the truth—who were satisfied with what they already believed.

3. John 7:17—To the closed-minded Jews who questioned His authority, Jesus said, "If any man will do his will, he shall know of the doctrine, whether it be of God, or whether I speak of myself." In other words, for the willing heart the truth is available. But they weren't willing. You say, "But how can people be like that?" The answer is simply stated in:

4. John 3:19—Men are like that because they love their sin. "Men loved darkness rather than light, because their deeds were evil." Because of their sin, the Pharisees didn't want to expose themselves. They were so smug in their self-righteousness and confirmed in willful ignorance that they turned their backs on the truth. That's tragic, because that puts them right into the category of those in:

5. Hebrews 10:29—Those who have heard enough information to believe the truth, but have rejected it, are going to receive punishment more severe than others: "Of how much sorer punishment, suppose ye, shall he be thought worthy, who hath trodden under foot the Son of God, and hath counted the blood of the covenant, with which he was sanctified, an

unholy thing." In other words, the greater punishment in hell is reserved for the people who knew the truth but trampled on it.

These Jews were so willfully ignorant:

B. Of Christ's Authority (vv. 25b-27)

"And Jesus saith unto them, Even the same that I said unto you from the beginning. I have many things to say and to judge of you; but he that sent me is true; and I speak to the world those things which I have heard of him. They understood not that he spoke to them of the Father."

Because these Jews refused to accept what Jesus had been saying, Jesus doesn't provide them with any further revelation. But He does say that He has words of judgment to speak concerning them, which come from the Father, who "hath committed all judgment unto the Son" (John 5:22b). Willful ignorance brings judgment, as do unbelief, earthbound attitudes, and self-righteousness, and the Pharisees were characterized by all of them. In their spiritual blindness, they didn't recognize who He was or understand that He spoke to them about God the Father. They just thought He was talking about some judgment on His own part. They did not understand what He was talking about, and yet He had made it clear again and again. Judgment is a terrible result for those who continually refuse to hear the truth. That is why Jesus warned, "Who hath ears to hear, let him hear" (Matt. 13:9).

The Jews also gave evidence of their willful ignorance:

C. Of Christ's Immortality (v. 28)

"Then said Jesus unto them, When ye have lifted up the Son of man, then shall ye know that I am he, and that I do nothing of myself; but as my Father hath taught me, I speak these things."

"How were the Jews going to know that?" you ask. Well, what did the Father do at the death of Christ to verify the claims He had made? He raised Him from the dead. Repeatedly the Bible teaches that. In effect, Jesus says, "When My resurrection comes, then you are going to have to look honestly at My claims." And do you know what happened? Many of the Jews did. When it became known that Jesus had been resurrected, the church was born, and literally thousands of people in the city of Jerusalem did see the truth and believe, didn't they? There was a great response. Maybe out of the very crowd before Jesus there were some people who later became a part of that early church.

Finally, the statement in verse 29 shows that many of the Jews were willfully ignorant:

D. Of Christ's Unity (v. 29)

"And he that sent me is with me. The Father hath not left me alone; for I do always those things that please him."

The Pharisees could not comprehend Christ's unity with God. So Jesus says, "You are going to know the Father is with Me and has sent Me and that all the claims I made are true, in the day that I am lifted up to be crucified, because the result of death is going to be the resurrection." But for then, they didn't know. And many of them never knew and consequently died in their sins, to be separated from God for eternity.

Conclusion

It's not possible, but I wish we could transport ourselves back in a time capsule and meet those people so that we could understand the tragedy of rejecting Christ. You would get a little idea of the intensity and the fearfulness of such a warning as Jesus made here. Those self-righteous, earthbound, unbelieving, and willfully ignorant Jews didn't need to die in their sins—there was and is another option: "As he spoke these words, many believed on him" (John 8:30). Aren't you glad for that?

You can't always preach the positives—you have to preach the negatives, because the negatives are needed to bring some folks to Christ. If you have never committed yourself to Jesus Christ, you are separated from Him by a gulf that you could never ever span on your own. Not all of your good deeds, self-righteousness, or religion could do it. The only way that gulf can be spanned is for you to recognize your sin and receive the Lord Jesus Christ. If you have a desire in your heart to do that today, just simply pray something like, "God, I want Jesus Christ as my Savior. I receive Him now. I don't want to die in my sin. I want to go where You are." And if you do that in sincerity, He will hear that prayer, and your life will be "translated . . . into the kingdom of his dear Son" (Col. 1:13b). If your faith is weak, ask Him to help you believe. If you need more information so that you can make that decision, and you truly want to know Him, ask God to teach you the truth about Christ.

Focusing on the Facts

1. What are some positive results of coming to Christ (see p. 99)?
2. What is the result of not receiving Jesus Christ (see p. 99)?
3. Can a person remain neutral rather than choose to follow Christ? What did Jesus imply about choosing in Matthew 12:30 (see p. 100)?

4. Why are some men condemned, according to John 3:18 (see p. 100)?
5. Who does the Bible say is responsible when a person goes to hell? Why (see p. 101)?
6. For what two reasons did Jesus say that the Jews should believe Him (John 14:10-11; see p. 101)?
7. Why did the crowds initially follow Christ? Why did many later on no longer want to crown Him King (see p. 102)?
8. What is the tragic result of refusing to believe in Jesus Christ (see p. 103)?
9. What did Jesus probably have in mind when He tells the Pharisees in John 8:21 that they will die in their sin (see p. 103)?
10. Where were the Jewish leaders seeking for heaven? Where should they have been seeking it (see p. 104)?
11. What is one way for a person to die in his sin? Why are these people the hardest to reach with the truth of the gospel (see p. 105)?
12. Upon what are the phony religious systems that Satan puts together based (see p. 106)?
13. What did the Jews conclude about the reason they would be unable to go where Jesus was going (see pp. 106-107)?
14. Rather than suicide, what type of death did Jesus die (see p. 107)?
15. What is the big lie of Satan? What does it contradict (see p. 107)?
16. What is the attitude that accompanies self-righteousness (see pp. 107-108)?
17. Who did Jesus imply that the Jews followed when He told them that they were "from beneath" (John 8:23a)? From where are believers guided (see pp. 108-109)?
18. To what does "this world" refer in the context of John 8:23? What are some of its characteristics? What is the world's eventual destiny, according to 1 John 2:17 (see p. 109)?
19. What is it that one must believe in order not to die in one's sins (see pp. 110-111)?
20. Who is the greater punishment in hell reserved for (Heb. 10:29; see p. 112)?
21. On whose authority was Jesus judging (see p. 113)?
22. What did the Father do at the death of Christ to verify the claims He had made (see p. 113)?
23. What was the positive response in Jerusalem that occurred as a result of the resurrection (see p. 113)?

Pondering the Principles

1. Do you know someone who is seeking for God in the wrong place and in the wrong way? Do you observe someone being tremendously committed to a system that is only a dead end, because it will never lead them into a true knowledge of God? Read Romans 10:1-4. What

attitude did Paul have, and what action did he take with regard to Israel, who had "a zeal for God, but not according to knowledge," according to verse 2? Of what was Israel ignorant? Using Paul's pattern, pray for that person whom you desire to see saved, asking that you might have an opportunity to show him or her that in Christ only is true righteousness found and granted to us by faith.

2. In sharing Christ with others, do you present the negatives as well as the positives? If you stated that Christ could change a person's life and give peace and joy, what might a professing Christian do when trials came in his life, according to such verses as Matthew 13:20-21? What might a non-Christian never do unless he is informed of the consequences of rejecting Christ? Observe in the following verses how Jesus mixed the negative with the positive: Matthew 13:45-50; John 12:44-50. As you share the gospel with others, make a commitment to tell them that the Christian life will not mean freedom from trials (2 Tim. 3:10-12) and that those who refuse to believe in Christ will die in their sin and be eternally separated from Christ (John 8:24; 2 Thess. 1:7-10).

Scripture Index

118

Moody Press, a ministry of the Moody Bible Institute, is designed for education, evangelization, and edification. If we may assist you in knowing more about Christ and the Christian life, please write us without obligation: Moody Press, c/o MLM, Chicago, Illinois 60610.